SMITHSONIAN INSTITUTION

UNITED STATES NATIONAL MUSEUM

BULLETIN 235

WASHINGTON, D.C.

1963

Publications of the United States National Museum

The scholarly publications of the United States National Museum include two series, *Proceedings of the United States National Museum* and *United States National Museum Bulletin*.

In these series are published original articles and monographs dealing with the collections and work of the Museum and setting forth newly acquired facts in the fields of Anthropology, Biology, History, Geology, and Technology. Copies of each publication are distributed to libraries and scientific organizations and to specialists and others interested in the different subjects.

The *Proceedings*, begun in 1878, are intended for the publication, in separate form, of shorter papers. These are gathered in volumes, octavo in size, with the publication date of each paper recorded in the table of contents in the volume.

In the *Bulletin* series, the first of which was issued in 1875, appear longer, separate publications consisting of monographs (occasionally in several parts) and volumes in which are collected works on related subjects. *Bulletins* are either octavo or quarto in size, depending on the needs of the presentation. Since 1902 papers relating to the botanical collections of the Museum have been published in the *Bulletin* series under the heading *Contributions from the United States National Herbarium*.

This work is number 235 of the *Bulletin* series.

FRANK A. TAYLOR
Director, United States National Museum

For sale by the Superintendent of Documents, U.S. Government Printing Office
Washington 25, D.C. - Price $2

Shoulder-belt plate of Vermont Militia, attributed to Ethan Allen, about 1785. In collection of Dr. John Lattimer.

MUSEUM OF HISTORY AND TECHNOLOGY

American Military Insignia
1800–1851

J. Duncan Campbell and Edgar M. Howell

SMITHSONIAN INSTITUTION, WASHINGTON, D.C.

1963

Contents

Preface

This catalog is a descriptive and interpretive listing of the insignia of the Army of the United States—other than buttons, epaulets, and horse furniture—in the National Collections that were prescribed or worn during the period 1800–1851. The subject of early American military buttons has been covered by L. F. Emilio in *The Emilio Collection of Military Buttons* (Salem, Massachusetts: Essex Institute, 1911), W. L. Calver and R. P. Bolton in *History Written with Pick and Shovel* (New York: New York Historical Society, 1950), and David F. Johnson in *Uniform Buttons, American Armed Forces, 1784–1948.* (Watkins Glen, New York: Century House, 1948, 2 vols.). For epaulets, see Mendel L. Peterson, "American Army Epaulets, 1814–1872," *Military Collector and Historian* (March 1961, vol. 3, no. 1, pp. 1–14).

Most of the specimens described here are from the huge W. Stokes Kirk Collection acquired in 1959, supplemented by the War Department Collection and the numerous biographical collections of the United States National Museum; in addition, a few insignia in the collections of J. Duncan Campbell and others are included.

The unique W. Stokes Kirk Collection, unmatched in scope, volume, and rarity, is worthy of special note. It was begun in 1878 by W. Stokes Kirk, Sr., of Philadelphia, a dealer in U.S. Government surplus. Struck by the beautiful design and delicate art work in some of the early insignia, Mr. Kirk put aside all old and unusual devices for his personal collection. As his business expanded, so did his interest in military rarities and curios. After each bulk purchase from government sources, he would have all the odd and unusual items sorted out for his examination. The best of such items went into his personal collection, which included rare firearms, powder flasks, insignia, epaulets, military caps, and the like. W. Stokes Kirk, Jr., who succeeded his father and expanded the business nationally until it became almost as well known as Bannerman's Military Store in New York City, maintained and enlarged the collection. After his death, in 1946, the collection was continued by his widow, Mrs. Linnie A. Kirk Mosler. Items in this catalog from the W. Stokes Kirk Collection are indicated by the letters "S–K" in parentheses following the United States National Museum number.

Although this catalog is, in more than one sense, a developmental history of American military insignia, it is not, and is not intended to be, a definitive study. The picture is far too incomplete. Whereas the record of Regular Army devices after 1821 is fairly clear—despite the fact that the uniform regulations continued sometimes to use the tantalizing phrase "according to pattern"—there remain serious gaps in the pre-1821 period when regulations were exceedingly vague and fragmentary at best;

for example, the badges of the Regiment of Light Artillery (1812–1821). These gaps will be filled only by excavating at sites known to have been occupied by specific Regular units during particular periods. Indeed, since this study was begun, four unique and significant insignia were excavated at the site of a War of 1812 cantonment, and these greatly enrich our knowledge of the period.

The record of insignia of the veritable multitude of independent uniformed Militia companies in existence during the period under consideration may never be complete. The selection presented here, however, is an excellent representative chronological cross section of typical designs and variations of insignia worn by the uniformed or "volunteer" Militia, as opposed to the "common" or "standing" Militia.

The best sources of documentation and dating for Regular Army devices are the uniform regulations and ordnance regulations; these are supplemented by pertinent records in the National Archives, notably the letter files of the Purveyor of Public Supplies and of the Commissary General of Purchases. The letter files are voluminous, but in some cases badly mixed and in many cases incomplete. We have conjectured a reason for this incompleteness. The two prime contractors for military insignia during the period 1812–1821 were George Armitage and William Crumpton, both of whom had their small factories in Philadelphia within a mile of the office of Callendar Irvine, Commissary General of Purchases. The paucity of written transactions in the records in the National Archives between these gentlemen and Irvine tends to bear out our assumption that most of their dealings were conducted verbally in Irvine's office. This would account for the lack of sketches and drawings of cap plates and belt plates in files of the National Archives. In cases where no specific documentary evidence is available, dating has been based on a careful evaluation of design development and comparison with biographical specimens that can be more fairly dated through knowledge of the former owner's career. Excavated insignia from datable sites have also reduced the problem considerably.

For Militia insignia worn about 1835, the best documentation is to be found in *U.S. Military Magazine*, published between 1839 and 1842 by Huddy and Duval of Philadelphia, and in *New York Military Magazine*, published by Labree and Stockton of New York during 1841. In 1939, Frederick P. Todd described the Huddy and Duval prints in detail (*Journal of the American Military Institute*, 1939, vol. 3, no. 3, pp. 166–176). However, evaluation and consideration of over-all design development and comparison with dated biographical specimens of the earlier period, before 1835, are difficult and must be done cautiously, as there is no orderly pattern. One generalization does seem clear: during the decade after 1821, when the Regulars discarded large cap plates, the Militia almost universally adopted them and continued to wear them well into the 1840's. Very few insignia include the maker's name or initials, but when they do, bracketing within a definite period is relatively easy. Similarly, when a cap plate appears to be original to a cap, the design of the cap and its maker's label, if included, are of great help. Finally, when there is nothing else to rely on, the "feel" of the specimen, gained through the experience of studying several thousand, has been used, although with reluctance.

The year 1800 was selected as the opening date of the study because it was in that year that the first metal ornament was prescribed to designate a particular branch of service. The closing date of 1851 was chosen because Regular Army devices for that year and thereafter are well documented in uniform regulations, manuals, and catalogs of manufacturers such as William Horstmann and Sons. Militia dress after that general date becomes so increasingly complex that it should be attempted only as a separate study.

Most of the specimens described in this study were struck from steel dies; however—despite the relative wealth of knowledge on the striking of coins—little is known of the exact process, especially prior to the appearance of the punch press in the 1830's. Several insignia dies dating as early as the War of 1812 period and a number dating in the 1840's do exist, however. All of these examined were found to be female dies, with the design in intaglio rather than in relief. The design was worked into the die—the art generally termed "die-sinking"—in the same basic manner as in coin dies. The die sinker first softened the steel to suit his particular taste and then incised the design, using a succession of small chisels. The steel was then retempered to withstand high impact pressures. Although there is no documentation on the subject, manufacturing techniques of the period indicate that the following process was probably employed: the die was locked in place at the base of a drop press, similar to a guillotine, so that it could be struck accurately from above; a piece of pure lead was then affixed to the bottom of the weighted drop and allowed to strike the die a sufficient number of times to completely receive the impression of the die and become, in effect, a male counterpart; lastly, a thin sheet of brass, copper, or pewter was placed on the female die and struck with the weighted lead male, receiving the desired impression but without the excessive stretching and resultant cracking that a steel-on-steel strike might have produced. Examination of finished products in the national collections bears out this theory of production; few if any of the specimens show evidence of having been struck with a steel male die.

With only a few exceptions, all specimens have been photographed on a 1-inch grid. All references to right and left are made according to heraldic usage; the heraldic right is always on the left as viewed.

During the months this work has been in progress, many people and institutions have generously assisted in many ways. It is a pleasure to thank them for their help.

Mr. Detmar Finke of the Office of the Chief of Military History, Department of the Army, reviewed the Regular Army portions of the manuscript and made many valuable suggestions. Mr. Frederick P. Todd, director of The West Point Museum, graciously answered many questions relative to both Regular Army and Militia insignia. Through the courtesy of Mr. James Koping and Miss Elizabeth Ulrich of the Pennsylvania State Library, The *U.S. Military Magazine* of Huddy and Duval was made available for unlimited use.

Thanks are also given to the following, who furnished photographs of specimens in their collections: Mr. Waverly P. Lewis, Devon, Connecticut; Mr. William E. Codd, Monkton, Maryland; The Filson Club, Louisville, Kentucky; The West Point Museum; The Fort Sill Museum; Old Fort Erie Museum, Ontario, Canada; The Niagara Historical Society Museum, Niagara-on-the-Lake, Ontario, Canada; The Washington County Historical Society Museum, Fort Calhoun, Nebraska; the Valley Forge Chapel Museum, and Dr. John Lattimer, New York City.

Mr. Michael Arpad of Washington, D.C., was especially helpful in matters pertaining to the techinques of chasing and die sinking.

J. Duncan Campbell
Edgar M. Howell

March 1, 1963.

Bibliography

The following works have been used in gathering the material for this book. They are frequently referred to in the text in shortened form.

American military history, 1607–1953. (ROTC Manual 145–20, Department of the Army.) Washington, 1956.

American state papers, class V, military affairs. Vol. 1. Washington: Gales and Seaton, 1832.

ANSELL, S. T. Legal and historical aspects of the Militia. *Yale Law Journal* (April 1917), vol. 26, no. 6, pp. 471–480.

BARNES, R. M. *Military uniforms of Britain and the Empire.* London: Seeley Service and Co., 1960.

BELOTE, THEODORE T. *American and European swords in the historical collections of the United States National Museum.* (U.S. National Museum Bulletin 163.) Washington, 1932.

A bit of U.S. Mint history. *American Journal of Numismatics* (1908), vol. 43, no. 2, pp. 45–50.

CALVER, W. L., and BOLTON, R. P. *History written with pick and shovel.* New York: New York Historical Society, 1950.

CHAMBERLAIN, GEORGIA S. Moritz Furst, die-sinker and artist. *The Numismatist* (June 1954), vol. 67, no. 6, pp. 588–592.

DAVIS, GHERARDI. *The colors of the United States Army, 1789–1912.* New York: Privately printed, 1912.

EMILIO, L. F. *The Emilio collection of military buttons.* Salem, Massachusetts: Essex Institute, 1911.

FINKE, DETMAR H. Insignia of rank in the Continental Army, 1775 1783. *Military Collector and Historian* (fall 1956), vol. 8, no. 3, pp. 71–73.

General regulations for the Army. Philadelphia: M. Carey and Sons, 1821.

General regulations for the Army of the United States. Washington: Department of the Army, 1835.

General regulations for the Army of the United States, 1847. Washington: J. and G. S. Gideon, 1847.

GRONERT, T. G. The first national pastime in the Middle West. *Indiana Magazine of History* (September 1933), vol. 29, no. 3, pp. 171–186.

History of the organization of the United States cavalry. MS, Office of the Chief of Military History, Department of the Army, Washington, D.C.

HOPKINS, ALFRED F. Volunteer corps hat of 1814. *Military Affairs* (winter 1941), vol. 5, no. 4, pp. 271–272.

JOHNSON, DAVID F. *Uniform buttons, American armed forces, 1784–1948.* 2 vols. Watkins Glen, New York: Century House, 1948.

JONES, WILLARD L. History of the organization of the United States Field Artillery. MS, Office of the Chief of Military History, Department of the Army, Washington, D.C.

Journals of the Continental Congress, 1774–1789. Edit. Worthington Chauncey Ford and others. 34 vols. Washington: Carnegie Foundation, 1904–1937.

KIVETT, MARVIN F. Excavations at Fort Atkinson, Nebraska, a preliminary report. *Nebraska History* (March 1959), vol. 40, no. 1, pp. 39–66.

Knox papers. MSS Division, Library of Congress, Washington, D.C.

KUHN, EDWARD C. U.S. Army colors and standards of 1808. *Military Affairs* (winter 1941), vol. 5, no. 4, pp. 263–267.

LEFFERTS, CHARLES W. *Uniforms of the American, British, French, and German Armies in the War of the American Revolution.* New York: New York Historical Society, 1926.

LEWIS, WAVERLY P. *U.S. military headgear, 1770–1880.* Devon, Connecticut: Privately printed, 1960.

LUNDEBERG, PHILIP K. A history of the North Carolina Militia, 1784–1848. Master's dissertation, Duke University, 1947.

MAHON, JOHN K. The citizen soldier in national defense, 1789–1815. Doctor's dissertation, University of California at Los Angeles, 1950.

——. History of the organization of the United States Infantry. (Pp. 1–61 in vol. 2 of *The Army lineage book,* Washington: Department of the Army, 1953.)

McBARRON, H. CHARLES. Regiment of Riflemen, winter uniform, 1812–1815. *Military Collector and Historian* (December 1954), vol. 6, no. 4, p. 100.

——. The 18th U.S. Infantry Regiment, 1814–1815. *Military Collector and Historian* (summer 1955), vol. 7, no. 2, pp. 48–49.

McCLELLAN, E. N. Uniforms of the American Marines, 1775 to 1827. Mimeographed in 1932 by Marine Corps Historical Section, Department of the Navy, Washington, D.C.

The military laws of the United States. Edit. John F. Callan. Philadelphia: George W. Childes, 1863.

New York Military Magazine (1841).

Official Army register, corrected to October 31, 1848. Washington, 1848.

Official drawings for the U.S. Army uniform regulations of 1851. *Military Collector and Historian,* vol. 10, no. 1 (spring 1958), pp. 17–19; vol. 10, no. 2 (summer 1958), pp. 43–45.

Old Print Shop Portfolio (May 1961), vol. 20, no. 9.

PARKYN, MAJ. H. G. *Shoulder-belt plates and buttons.* Aldershot, Hants, England: Gale and Polden, Ltd., 1956.

PATTERSON, C. MEADE. The military rifle flasks of 1832 and 1837. *Military Collector and Historian* (March 1953), vol. 5, no. 1, pp. 7–12.

PETERSON, HAROLD L. *The American sword,* New Hope, Pennsylvania: The River House, 1954.

PETERSON, MENDEL L. American Army epaulets, 1841–1872. *Military Collector and Historian* (March 1951), vol. 3, no. 1, pp. 1–14.

PREBLE, GEORGE HENRY. *History of the flag of the United States of America.* Boston: A. Williams and Co., 1880.

Records of the Adjutant General's Office. Record Group 94, National Archives, Washington, D.C.

Regulations for the government of the Ordnance Department. Washington: Francis P. Blair, 1834.

Regulations for the uniform and dress of the Army of the United States, June 1851. Philadelphia: William H. Horstmann and Sons, 1851.

RIKER, WILLIAM H. *Soldiers of the States.* Washington: Public Affairs Press, 1957.

Standing Order Book, 1st Infantry, Detroit. MSS Division, Library of Congress, Washington, D. C.

SWANSON, NEIL H. *The perilous flight.* New York: Farrar and Rinehart, 1945.

TODD, FREDERICK P. The Huddy and Duval prints. *Journal of the American Military Institute* (1939). vol. 3, no. 3, pp. 166-176.

————. Notes on the dress of the Regiment of Light Artillery, U.S.A. *Military Collector and Historian* (March 1950), vol. 2, no. 1, p. 10.

————. Our National Guard: An introduction to its history. *Military Affairs*, vol. 5, no. 2 (summer 1941), pp. 73–86; vol. 5, no. 3 (fall 1941), pp. 152–170.

————. The curious case of the Voltigeur uniform. *Military Collector and Historian* (June 1952), vol. 4, no. 2, pp. 44–45.

————. Notes on the organization and uniforms of South Carolina military forces, 1860–1861. *Military Collector and Historian* (September 1951), vol. 3, no. 3, pp. 53–62.

————. Three leather cockades. *Military Collector and Historian* (spring 1956), vol. 8, no. 1, pp. 24–25.

TOWNSEND, F. C., and TODD, FREDERICK P. Branch insignia of the Regular cavalry, 1833–1872. *Military Collector and Historian* (spring 1956), vol. 8, no. 1, pp. 1–5.

UPTON, EMORY. The military policy of the United States. Senate Document No. 379, 64th Congress, 1st Session. Washington: 1916.

U.S. Military Magazine (1839–1842), vols. 1–3.

WALL, ALEXANDER J. The flag with an eagle in the canton. *New York Historical Society Quarterly Bulletin* (October 1933), vol. 17, no. 3, pp. 51–67.

WIKE, JOHN W. Untitled MS, Office of the Chief of Military History, Department of the Army, Washington, D.C.

Writings of George Washington. Edit. John G. Fitzpatrick. Washington: 1944.

ZIEBER, EUGENE. *Heraldry in America.* Philadelphia: Bailey, Banks, and Biddle, 1909.

American Military Insignia
1800-1851

Introduction

*I*N ALMOST ALL ARMIES it long has been standard practice to use distinctive devices of cloth and metal to distinguish between arms and services, and between individual units of each arm, to enhance morale and develop esprit de corps. Colors of units of the British Army have had ancient badges emblazoned on them since before the establishment of the present standing army in 1661. By the end of the first half of the 18th century some of these badges had been authorized for placement on horse furniture or for wear on grenadier caps. This was especially true of the regiments of horse and a few of the older regiments of foot. The infantry regiments received numerical designations in 1751, and these numbers were worn on waist belts, shoulder belts, and cartridge-box plates. When the infantry units acquired county titles in 1782, these names often were added to the plates. In 1767 regimental numbers were ordered placed on the buttons of officers and other ranks; in practice these numbers were often combined with other devices. [1]

In the American Army such devices have taken many forms, ranging from distinctive buttons, plumes, cockades, cap plates, shoulder-belt plates, and waist-belt and cartridge-box plates to the well-known shoulder sleeve insignia and distinctive unit insignia of the present day. The origin of much of this insignia and many of the changes in its design can be tied more or less directly to the organization of the Regular Army—its contractions and expansions and its changes in arm and service designations—and to the peculiar circumstances surrounding the origin and growth of the volunteer or uniformed Militia. Thus, a short discussion of the organization of each is in order. [2]

Organization of the Regular Army

Two months after the War of the Revolution officially ended with the signing of a peace treaty on September 3, 1783, General Washington directed the Army to turn in its arms and disband. [3] Since the Continental Congress had made no provision for a permanent establishment, Washington retained in service one infantry regiment and a battalion of artillery to guard military stores and take over posts to be evacuated by the British. [4] Early in June 1784 Congress ordered these units disbanded except for

---

[1] PARKYN's *Shoulder-Belt Plates and Buttons* contains a wealth of information on British regimental devices.

[2] For history of the organization of the Army, see *American Military History, 1607–1953;* MAHON, "History of the Organization of the United States Infantry"; and JONES, "History of the Organization of the United States Field Artillery."

Unfortunately, there is no single, completely satisfactory source on the militia system of the United States. The following works, however, contain sound information and, when taken together, provide an excellent background on the subject: TODD, "Our National Guard"; MAHON, "Citizen Soldier"; LUNDEBERG, "History of the North Carolina Militia"; ANSELL, "Legal and Historical Aspects of the Militia"; GRONERT, "First National Pastime in the Middle West"; and RIKER, *Soldiers of the States.*

[3] *Writings of George Washington,* vol. 27, p. 222.

[4] Ibid., pp. 256–258; also letter dated January 3, 1784, from Henry Knox, Commander in Chief of the Army, to President of the Continental Congress (in Knox papers).

detachments to guard stores at Fort Pitt and West Point; then, in order to secure the frontier against Indian unrest, it immediately authorized a regiment to be raised from the militia of four of the States to comprise eight companies of infantry and two of artillery.[5] This unit, called the First American Regiment, gradually turned into a regular organization.

The failure of an expedition commanded by Col. Josiah Harmar of the First American Regiment against the Indians in 1790 awakened the Congress somewhat to the threat in the Northwest and resulted in the organization of another infantry regiment, which was designated the 2d Infantry Regiment; the First American Regiment was redesignated the "1st".[6] Trouble with the Indians continued, and after another severe reverse Congress authorized the raising of three additional infantry regiments and, at the same time, empowered the President to organize the Army as he might see fit.[7]

Under this discretionary power, the Army was reorganized into the Legion of the United States. This was a field army in which the three combat branches—infantry, cavalry, and artillery—were combined. The Legion was in turn broken down into four sublegions, with each containing infantry, cavalry, artillery, and riflemen; thus, the sublegions were the fore-runners of the modern combined arms team. The 1st and 2d Infantries became the 1st and 2d Sublegions. Of the three additional infantry regiments authorized, only two were organized, these becoming the 3d and 4th Sublegions.[8] Under the forceful leadership of Gen. Anthony Wayne the Legion reversed the record on the frontier and decisively defeated the Indians at the Battle of Fallen Timbers. The temporary peace which followed turned attention to the problem of protecting the Atlantic seaboard, and in 1794 Congress authorized a large increase in the artillery, assigned engineer officers, and designated the new organization the Corps of Artillerists and Engineers.[9] The Legion was continued until it was replaced in 1796 by the 1st, 2d, 3d, and 4th Infantry Regiments, which were constituted from the four sublegions, two troops of light dragoons, and the above-mentioned Corps.[10]

The threat of war with France in 1798 brought further expansions. In April of that year an "additional regiment" of artillerists and engineers was authorized, with the Corps created in 1794 becoming the 1st and the new unit being designated the 2d Regiment of Artillerists and Engineers.[11] In the following July, 12 more regiments of infantry and 6 troops of light dragoons—to be combined with the two troops in existence to form a regiment—were authorized; an additional 24 regiments of infantry, plus units of other arms, authorized the following winter made a total of 40 regiments of infantry.[12] Actually, the greatest part of this force remained on paper. Only the 1st and 2d Infantries ever attained their required strength, and only 3,400 men were enlisted for the 5th through the 16th. There were no enlistments at all for the other regiments. Officers were assigned to the six troops of light dragoons, but no enlisted personnel were raised and no horses were bought.[13]

More quickly than it had arisen, the threat of a war with France abated. Early in 1800 action was suspended under the two acts creating the paper regiments, and the Army was reduced to the regular establishment of four regiments of infantry, two regiments of artillerists and engineers, and two troops of light dragoons.[14] Two years later the antipathy of the new Jefferson administration to a standing army further reduced this establishment to two regiments of infantry and one of artillery. The Corps of Artillerists and Engineers was abolished; a Corps of Engineers was organized to be stationed at West Point and "constitute a military academy"; and the light dragoons were disbanded.[15]

The Jeffersonian theories regarding a strong militia and a small professional army were rudely shaken in 1807 by the *Chesapeake-Leopard* affair. With war seeming imminent, Congress added to the Regular Establishment, though cautiously "for a limited time," five regiments of infantry, one regiment of riflemen, one of light artillery, and one of light dragoons. The new regiments of infantry were numbered the 3d through

---

[5] Journals of the Continental Congress, vol. 27, p. 524; also, UPTON, p. 69.
[6] Act of March 3, 1791 (*Military Laws*, pp. 90–91).
[7] Act of March 5, 1792 (*Military Laws*, pp. 92–94).
[8] *American State Papers*, pp. 40–41.
[9] Act of May 9, 1794 (*Military Laws*, p. 104).
[10] Act of May 30, 1796 (*Military Laws*, p. 114).

[11] Act of April 27, 1798 (*Military Laws*, pp. 119–120).
[12] Acts of July 16, 1798, and March 2, 1799 (*Military Laws*, pp. 127–128).
[13] *American State Papers*, p. 137.
[14] Acts of February 20 and May 14, 1800 (*Military Laws*, pp. 139, 141); also, *American State Papers*, p. 139.
[15] Act of March 16, 1802 (*Military Laws*, pp. 141–149).

the 7th.[16] There was no further preparation for a fight with England until just before war was actually declared. In January 1812, 10 regiments of infantry, two of artillery, and one regiment of light dragoons were added; three months later a Corps of Artificers was organized; and in June provision was made for eight more infantry regiments, making a total of 25.[17] In January 1813, following the discouragements of the early campaigns in the Northwest, Congress constituted 20 more infantry regiments, bringing the total to 45, the largest number in the Regular Establishment until the 20th century.[18] A year later three more regiments of riflemen, designated the 2d through the 4th, were formed.[19]

In March 1814 Congress reorganized both the artillery and the dragoons. The three artillery regiments, which had never operated as such, but rather by company or detachment, were consolidated into the Corps of Artillery; and the two regiments of dragoons, which had never been adequately trained and generally had given a poor account of themselves, were merged into one.[20] The Regiment of Light Artillery remained untouched.

Almost as soon as the war ended, Congress moved to reduce the Army [21] by limiting the peacetime establishment to 10,000 men, to be divided among infantry, artillery, and riflemen, plus the Corps of Engineers. The number of wartime infantry units was reduced to eight, and the rifle units to one. The

Corps of Artillery and the Regiment of Light Artillery were retained, but dragoons were eliminated.[22]

By 1821 the prospects of a prolonged peace appeared so good that Congress felt safe in further reducing the Army. Consequently, in that year the number of infantry regiments was cut to seven; the Rifle Regiment was disbanded; the Corps of Artillery and the Regiment of Light Artillery were disbanded, with four artillery regiments being organized in their stead; and the Ordnance Department was merged with the artillery,[23] an arrangement that continued until 1832.

The opening of the West in the decades following the War of 1812 brought an important change in the organization of the Army. Experience having shown that infantry were at a distinct disadvantage when pitted against the fleetly mounted Indians, in 1832 a battalion of mounted rangers was organized to quell disturbances on the northwest frontier,[24] but this loosely knit force was replaced by a regiment of dragoons the following year.[25] The mounted arm had come to stay in the Army.

When the second Seminole War broke out in 1836, a second regiment of dragoons was organized. [26] And, as the war dragged through another inconclusive year, a reluctant Congress was forced to increase the size of existing line units and to authorize an additional regiment of infantry, the 8th. Meanwhile, increasing demands for surveying and mapping services resulted in the creation of the Corps of Topographical Engineers as a separate entity.[27]

Meanwhile, the responsibilities of the Army in the opening of the West continued to increase, and in 1846 the Regiment of Mounted Riflemen was organized to consolidate the northern route to the Pacific by establishing and manning a series of posts along the Oregon Trail.[28] However, the outbreak of the War with Mexico postponed this mission.

At the start of the War with Mexico Congress leaned heavily on volunteer units, with the hard

---

[16] Act of April 12, 1808 (*Military Laws*, pp. 200–203).

[17] Acts of January 11, April 23, and June 26, 1812 (*Military Laws*, pp. 212–215, 222–223, 230).

[18] Act of January 1813 (*Military Laws*, pp. 238–240). There is some confusion as to just how many infantry regiments were organized and actually came into being. The Act of January 29, 1813, authorized the President to raise such regiments of infantry as he should see fit, "not exceeding twenty." It seems that 19 were actually formed, made up partly of 1-year men and partly of 5-year men. There are 46 regiments listed in the Army Register for January 1, 1815, and it is known that several volunteer regiments were designated as units of the Regular Establishment and that a 47th and a 48th were redesignated as lower numbered units when several regiments were consolidated because of low recruitment rate. Mahon (in "History of the Organization of the United States Infantry") is not clear on this point. There is an organizational chart of the Army for this period in the files of the Office of the Chief of Military History, Department of the Army.

[19] Act of February 10, 1814 (*Military Laws*, pp. 251–252).

[20] Act of March 30, 1814 (*Military Laws*, pp. 252–255); JONES, p. 58; "History of the Organization of the United States Cavalry."

[21] Act of March 3, 1815 (*Military Laws*, pp. 266–267).

[22] The reorganization of 1815 is treated by MAHON "History of the Organization of the United States Infantry" (pp. 11–12), JONES "History of the Organization of the United States Field Artillery" (pp. 59–60), and WIKE, unpublished study.

[23] Act of March 2, 1821 (*Military Laws*, pp. 303–309).

[24] Acts of April 5 and June 15, 1832 (*Military Laws*, pp. 322–323, 325–326).

[25] Act of March 2, 1833 (*Military Laws*, pp. 329–330).

[26] Act of May 23, 1836 (*Military Laws*, pp. 336–337).

[27] Act of July 5, 1838 (*Military Laws*, pp. 341–349).

[28] Act of May 19, 1846 (*Military Laws*, pp. 371–372).

core of the Regulars remaining unchanged. But early in 1847 it was found necessary to add nine regiments of infantry and one regiment of dragoons.[29] Of the infantry units, eight were of the conventional type; the ninth was formed as the Regiment of Voltigeurs and Foot Riflemen. Theoretically, only half of this latter regiment was to be mounted. Each horseman was to be paired with a foot soldier who was to get up behind and ride double when speed was needed. In practice, however, none of the Voltigeurs were mounted; the entire unit fought as foot riflemen.[30]

All of these new units proved merely creatures of the war, and the coming of peace saw a reduction to the old establishment of eight regiments of infantry, four of artillery, two of dragoons, and one regiment of mounted riflemen.[31] This organization remained substantially unchanged until 1855.[32]

Organization of the Militia

The "common" Militia was first established by the various colonies of all able-bodied men between roughly the ages of 16 and 60 for protection against Indian attack. These militiamen were required by law to be enrolled in the unit of their township or county, furnish their own arms and equipment, and appear periodically for training. They were civilian soldiers who had little or no taste for things military, as their performance in both peace and war almost invariably demonstrated. They were not uniformed and contributed little or nothing to the field of military dress.

The "volunteer" or "independent" Militia companies, on the other hand, were something else again. These units, composed of men who enjoyed military life, or rather certain aspects of it, appeared rather early in the Nation's history. The first of these, formed in 1638, was The Military Company of the Massachusetts, later and better known as the Ancient and Honorable Artillery Company of Massachusetts. By 1750 there were a number of independent companies in existence—many of them chartered—and membership in them had become a recognized part of the social life of the larger urban centers.

The concept of volunteer Militia units was confirmed in the Uniform Militia Act of 1792, which prescribed flank companies of grenadiers, light infantry, or riflemen for the "common" Militia battalions and a company of artillery and a troop of horse for each division, to be formed of volunteers from the Militia at large and to be uniformed and equipped at the individual volunteer's expense. Thus, from within the national Militia structure emerged an elite corps of amateur—as opposed to civilian—soldiers who enjoyed military exercise, and the pomp and circumstance accompanying it, and who were willing to sacrifice both the time and the money necessary to enjoy it. Since the members were volunteers, they were ready to submit to discipline up to a point; they trained rather frequently; many of the officers made an effort to educate themselves militarily; they chose their own officers; and their relative permanency gave rise to an excellent esprit de corps. In actuality, these organizations became private military clubs, and differed from other male social and fraternal groups only in externals.

The great urban growth of the Nation during the period 1825–1860 was the golden age of the volunteer companies, and by 1845 these units had all but supplanted the common Militia. It would be difficult to even estimate the number of volunteer companies during this period. They sprang up almost everywhere, more in answer to a demand by the younger men of the Nation for a recreation that would meet a social and physical need and by emigrant minorities for a group expression than for reasons military. It was a "gay and gaudy" Militia, with each unit in its own distinctive and generally resplendent uniform. If the "Raleigh Cossacks," the "Hibernia Greens," the "Velvet Light Infantry Company," or the "Teutonic Rifles" were more "invincible in peace" than visible in war, they were a spectacular, colorful, and exciting integral of the social and military life of the first half of the 19th century

---

[29] Act of February 11, 1847 (*Military Laws*, pp. 379–382).

[30] MAHON, "History of the Organization of the United States Infantry," p. 16.

[31] Official Army Register, 1848.

[32] UPTON, p. 223.

6

Insignia of the Regular Army

Uniform regulations prior to 1821 were loosely and vaguely worded, and this was especially true in regard to officers' insignia. For example General Orders of March 30, 1800, stated: ". . . the swords of all officers, except the generals, to be attached by a white shoulder belt three inches wide, with an oval plate three inches by two and a half ornamented with an eagle." [33] In 1801 the 1st Infantry Regiment directed that "the sword . . . for platoon officers . . . be worn with a white belt over the coat with a breast plate such as have been by the Colonel established," [34] and in 1810 a regulation stated that "those gentlemen who have white sword belts and plates [are] to consider them as uniform, but those not so provided will be permitted to wear their waist belts." [35] As a result, the officers generally wore what they wished, and there was a wide variation in design. Most officer insignia were the product of local jewelers and silversmiths, although some known specimens are obviously the work of master craftsmen. Quality varied as well as design, depending on the affluence of the officer concerned. Some of the plainer plates appear to have been made by rolling silver dollars into an oval shape.

In regard to enlisted men's insignia, only the descriptions of the 1800 dragoon helmet plate and the 1814 and 1817 riflemen's cap plates give us anything approaching a clear picture. "Oblong silver plates . . . bearing the name of the corps and the number of the regiment" for the infantry in 1812, "plates in front" for the 1812 dragoons, and "gilt plate in front" for the 1812 light artillery are typical examples. As a result, the establishment of a proper chronology for these devices has depended on the careful consideration of specimens excavated at posts where specific units are known to have served at specific times, combined with research in pertinent records of the period in the National Archives.

Cap and Helmet Devices

DRAGOON HELMET PLATE, 1800

USNM 60330–M (S–K 86). Figure 1.

The first known distinctive metal branch insignia authorized for the Army was this helmet plate. General Order, U.S. Army, dated March 30, 1800, prescribed for "Cavalry . . . a helmet of leather crowned with black horse hair and having a brass front, with a mounted dragoon in the act of charging." [36] This oval plate, struck in thin brass with lead-filled back, has a raised rim, within which is a mounted, helmeted horseman in the act of charging; overhead is an eagle with a wreath in its beak. A double-wire fastener soldered to the back is not contemporary.

---

[33] General Orders, March 30, 1800 (Records AGO).
[34] Standing Order Book, folio 1, October 1, 1801.
[35] Records AGO.

---

[36] Records AGO.

FIGURE I

FIGURE 2

DRAGOON HELMET PLATE, 1800, DIE SAMPLE

USNM 60283–M (S–K 41). Figure 2.

Although from a different die, this plate, struck in thin brass, appears to be a die sample of the plate described above. It is also possible that it is a sample of the dragoon plate authorized in 1812.

¶ The 1813 uniform regulations specified for enlisted men of the artillery a "black leather cockade, with points 4 inches in diameter, a yellow button and eagle in the center, the button in uniform with the coat button." [37] This specification gives some validity to the belief that a cockade with an approximation of the artillery button tooled on it may also have been worn.

LEATHER COCKADE, ARTILLERY, C. 1808–1812

USNM 60256–M (S–K 14). Figure 3.

This cockade is of black leather of the size prescribed by the 1813 regulations. Tooled into the upper fan

is an eagle-on-cannon device with a stack of 6 cannon balls under the trail; an arc of 15 stars partially surrounds the eagle device. It is believed to have been worn on artillery *chapeaux de bras* as early as 1808.

The specimen is unmarked as to maker, but from correspondence of Callendar Irvine, Commissary General of Purchases from 1812 to 1841, it seems very possible that cockades similar to this one were made by Robert Dingee of New York City. Dingee is first listed in New York directories as a "saddler" (1812); he is listed later as "city weigher" (1828) and "inspector of green hides" (1831). The eagle-on-cannon design is similar to that of several Regular artillery buttons worn between 1802 and 1821, but it most closely approximates a button Johnson assigns to the period 1794–1810.[38]

¶ The question has been raised as to whether the Regulars ever wore a cockade with such a device. The 1813 and 1814 uniform regulations merely

---

[37] General Order, Southern Department, U.S. Army, January 24, 1813 (photostatic copy in files of division of military history, Smithsonian Institution); also, *American State Papers*, p. 434.

[38] Specimen no. 156 in JOHNSON, vol. 1, p. 43, vol. 2, pl. 9.

FIGURE 3

specified black leather cockades of 4 inches and 4½ inches in diameter respectively. However, since the Militia generally did not start adopting Regular Army devices until the 1820's it seems probable that this cockade was an item of Regular Army issue, despite the lack of evidence of specific authorization.

As early as January 1799 War Office orders specified: "All persons belonging to the Army, to wear a black cockade, with a small white eagle in the center. The cockade of noncommissioned officers, musicians, and privates to be of leather with Eagles of tin."[39] This regulation was repeated in 1800.[40] By 1802 these cockade eagles had taken the colors used for the buttons and lace of the different arms. The Purveyor of Public Supplies in that year purchased cockade eagles in tin (white) for infantry and in brass (yellow) for artillery enlisted men at a cost of one and two cents, respectively.[41] The cockade eagles of infantry officers were to be of silver and those of artillery

officers of gold. Cockades for company officers and enlisted personnel were to be of leather. The loosely worded regulation of 1813 infers that field officers' cockades might be of silk similar to the "black Ribbon" binding specified for their hats.[42]

It is extremely difficult to determine whether cockade eagles are of Regular Army or Militia origin, and to date them if the latter. They have been found in a wide variety of design and size, ranging from the rather plain example (fig. 6) to the highly refined one on the general officer's *chapeau de bras* (fig. 4). Examination of hats worn by both Regulars and Militia prior to 1821 reveals that there is little to choose between the eagles worn by the two components. After 1821, however, when Militia insignia tended to become more ornate and Regular devices more uniform, some of the Militia specimens emerge as distinct types because they have no Regular counterparts. Origin of the specimen, including excavations of military cantonment sites where the make-up of the garrison can be determined, has been the primary criterion used in assignment to either Regular Army or Militia, and to a lesser extent in dating. Over-all design and method of manufacture have also been considered in dating.

COCKADE EAGLE, GENERAL OFFICER, 1800–1812

USNM 12813. Figure 4.

Unusually refined in design, the eagle is of gold, with head to right, federal shield on breast, and olive branch in right talon. Three arrows, with points outward, are held in left talon.

This cockade eagle is on a *chapeau de bras* formerly belonging to Peter Gansevoort, brigadier general of the New York State Militia and brigadier general, U.S. Army, 1809–1812. Although Gansevoort wore this *chapeau* while serving as a Militia officer, as evidenced by a New York State button attached to it, this eagle is included with Regular Army devices because it is typical of those probably worn by high-ranking officers of both components.

---

[39] TODD, "Three Leather Cockades," pp. 24–25.

[40] General Order, March 30, 1800 (Records AGO).

[41] "Statement of Articles of Clothing, 1802," in papers of Purveyor of Public Supplies (Records AGO).

[42] General Order, Southern Department, U.S. Army, January 24, 1813 (photostatic copy in files of division of military history, Smithsonian Institution); also, *American State Papers*, p. 434.

FIGURE 4

COCKADE EAGLE, C. 1800–1821

USNM 60362–M (S–K 118).   Figure 5.

Cast in pewter and gold-finished, this eagle looks to the right, stands on clouds, and holds three arrows (facing inward) in the right talon and an upright olive branch in the left.

FIGURE 5

The eagle-on-clouds design is first seen on coins on the 1795 silver dollar.[43] It was popular during the

---

[43] Engraved by Robert Scott after a design by Gilbert Stuart.

War of 1812 period, and was not used in new designs by the Regular Army after 1821. Eagles of identical design and size are also known in pewter without finish. Such an eagle could have been worn by Militia as well as Regulars. Similar specimens have been excavated at Regular Army cantonment sites of the period.

COCKADE EAGLE, OFFICERS, 1800–1821

USNM 66352–M.   Figure 6.

This cockade eagle, which is struck in thin brass and silvered, was excavated on the site of a War of 1812 cantonment. Comparison with similar specimens in other collections indicates that the missing head was turned to the right. This eagle is classed as an officer's device because of its silvered brass composition. The elements comprising the arc on which the eagle stands cannot be identified because of the lightness of the strike.

¶ When the dragoons were disbanded in the 1802 reduction following the dissipation of the French scare, distinctive hat devices other than cockades

10

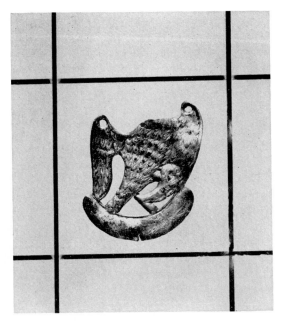

FIGURE 6

FIGURE 7.—Specimens in Campbell collection.

disappeared from the service. In 1808, when the Army was increased, the newly constituted regiments of light dragoons, light artillery, and riflemen were authorized to wear leather caps. The cap devices for these units were prescribed as Roman letters, "U.S.L.D.," "U.S.L.A.," and "U.S.R.R.," rather than plates. The letters were to be of brass, 1½ inches "in length."[44]

Illustrated in figure 7 are the letters "U" and "L", of brass, slightly more than 1 inch "in length" and a letter D,", of pewter, 1 inch "in length." The latter was excavated at Sackets Harbor, New York, where elements of the light artillery dragoons and riflemen are known to have served during 1813 and 1814. It seems obvious that pewter letters were worn by the dragoons as consonant with their other trimmings, for in July 1812 Col. James Burn of the 2d Light Dragoons requested official permission to issue such.[45]

With the large increase in the Army in 1812 came a change in the headgear of some corps and also a change in insignia. The light artillery was to wear a yoeman-crowned (i.e., wider at the crown than at the base) black cap with "gilt plate in front," and the infantry platoon officers and enlisted men were finally to have the black cylindrical caps (first prescribed in 1810) with "an oblong silver plate in front of the cap bearing the name of the corps and number of the regiment."[46] The rifle platoon officers and enlisted men were also to wear infantry caps, but with yellow trimmings.[47] The dragoons were authorized "helmets" with "plates" in 1812, and the foot artillery regiments in the fall of the same year were ordered to wear caps like the light artillery instead of the *chapeaux de bras* previously worn, which would have necessitated the use of plates.

The foot units received their new insignia almost immediately, the cap plates having been designed, contracted for, and delivered by late February 1812 for the 5th, 6th, 12th, and 15th Infantry Regiments[48]

[44] Todd, "Notes on the Dress," p. 10. Also, receipts from George Green and Son, and letter dated August 6, 1808, from J. Smith (Commissary General at Washington) to Tench Coxe requesting "brass letters U.S.R.R." (Records AGO). George Green is listed in Philadelphia directories of the period as a "brass founder and gilder."

[45] Letter dated July 8, 1812, from J. Burn to William Eustis (Secretary of War) and letter dated July 9, 1812, from B. Mifflin (Deputy Commissary General of Purchases). Both letters are in Records AGO.

[46] General Orders, January 24, 1813 (Records AGO).

[47] Letter dated March 30, 1812, from Coxe to Eustis (Records AGO); McBarron, "Regiment of Riflemen," p. 100.

[48] Bill dated February 24, 1812, from William Crumpton (Records AGO).

(the latter two were new units). This rapid action in regard to the infantry plates appears to be strong witness to the emphasis placed on distinctive insignia as morale factors and aids to enlistment, for active recruiting for the 10 new regiments did not begin until several months later. There were three different patterns of this infantry plate manufactured and issued, two of which are described below.

All arms were wearing cap plates by the middle of 1813, for there is record of such issue to the dragoons as well as record of rejection of ill-struck specimens for infantry, artillery, and rifles.[49] These plates were made variously by William Crumpton and George Armitage of Philadelphia, and Aaron M. Peasley of Boston.[50] Philadelphia directories list Crumpton as a button maker and silversmith between 1811 and 1822. Armitage is first listed in Philadelphia directories, in 1800, as a "silver plate worker"; in 1801 he is listed as "silverplater," and in 1820 as a "silverplater and military ornament maker." Peasley was an ornament and insignia maker in Boston during the same period.[51]

¶ The three types of infantry cap plates issued between 1812 and 1814 are somewhat similar, and all carry the prescribed "name of the corps and number of the regiment." All three specimens of these types are ground finds, two having been excavated after this work was in draft. The first pictured specimen (fig. 8, left) is believed to be the earliest pattern issued. Infantry plates as specified in the regulations were contracted for with William Crumpton late in 1811 or early 1812 by Tench Coxe, Purveyor of Public Supplies, and issued to troop units not later than the early summer.[52] They had been in use but a few months when their generally poor quality of composition forced several regimental commanders to complain to the new Commissary General of Purchases, Callendar Irvine, who had

just superseded Coxe, and to request something better. Irvine approved, and he let a contract for new plates with George Armitage of Philadelphia.[53] Irvine's reaction to the matter of the plates is an example of his opinion of his predecessor, Coxe, and Coxe's work in general, which he had observed while serving as Superintendent of Military Stores in Philadelphia. In replying to the complaint of Colonel Simonds, commanding officer of the 6th Infantry, Irvine wrote: "The plates are mere tin, in some respects like the man who designed and contracted for them, differing to him only as to durability . . . I am contracting for a plate of decent composition to issue with your next year's clothing."[54]

The first pattern carries the "name of the corps and the number of the regiment," the 15th Infantry, commanded by Col. Zebulon Pike who was one of the officers who complained to Irvine about the poor quality of cap plates. The specimen is of tinned iron and the letters and numerals have been struck with individual hand dies.

The two Armitage plates, very similar in over-all design (figures 8, right, and 9), have been designated the second and third patterns. At least one of these—perhaps both—apparently was designed by, and its die sunk by, Moritz Furst, well-known die sinker and designer of Philadelphia. On March 6, 1813, Irvine wrote the Secretary of War: "Mr. Furst executed a die for this office for striking infantry cap plates, designed by him, which has been admitted by judges to be equal, if not superior, to anything of the kind ever produced in this country."[55] Furst was Hungarian by birth. He studied design and die sinking at the mint in Vienna and came to the United States in 1807 with the expectation of becoming Chief Engraver at the Philadelphia Mint, an appointment which he did not receive. He sank the dies for many of the medals voted to War of 1812 leaders, did the obverse die work for a number of Indian peace medals, and is believed to have designed the swords given by the State of New York to Generals Brown, Scott, Gaines, and Macomb.[56]

[49] Letter dated August 31, 1812, from Eustis to Irvine; General Order of January 24, 1813, Southern Department; letter dated March 31, 1813, from Irvine to Amasa Stetson (Deputy Commissary General of Purchases, Boston); and letter dated July 13, 1813, from Irvine to M. T. Wickham. This material is in Records AGO.

[50] Letter from Irvine to Wickham dated July 13, 1813, and bill from William Crumpton dated February 24, 1812 (both in Records AGO).

[51] Statement of purchases for September 1813, by Stetson (Records AGO).

[52] Bill dated February 24, 1812, from William Crumpton (Records AGO).

[53] Letter dated November 8, 1812, from Irvine to Colonel Simonds (Commanding Officer, 6th Infantry); letter dated November 3, 1812, from Irvine to Colonel Pike (Commanding Officer, 15th Infantry); and letter dated November 23, 1812, from Irvine to Armitage. These letters are in Records AGO.

[54] Letter from Irvine to Simonds cited in preceding note.

[55] Letter in Records AGO.

[56] "A Bit of U.S. Mint History," pp. 45–50; and CHAMBERLAIN, pp. 588–592.

FIGURE 8, left.

FIGURE 8, right.

CAP PLATE, INFANTRY, 1812

USNM 66456–M. *Figure 8, right.*

This is the second pattern of the infantry cap plate described in the 1812 regulations as an "oblong silver plate . . . bearing the name of the corps and the number of the regiment." The specimen was excavated on the site of Smith's Cantonment at Sackets Harbor, New York, known to have been occupied by Regular infantry during the 1812–1815 period. The piece is struck in "white metal" and tinned [the term "silver" in the regulation referred only to color]. It is rectangular, with clipped corners, and is dominated by an eagle, with wings outspread, grasping lightning bolts in the right talon and an olive branch in the left talon. Below is a panoply of stacked arms, flags with 6-pointed stars, two drums, and a cartridge box marked "u.s." The corps designation "u.s. infantry" is above; the unit designation is blank with the letters "regt." on the left. The plate is pierced with four pairs of holes on each side for attachment.

Another example of this second pattern is known; it is attached to an original cap and bears the unit designation "12 regt."

CAP PLATE, INFANTRY, 1812 (REPRODUCTION)

USNM 60249 (S–K 7). *Figure 9.*

This is the third pattern of the infantry cap plate prescribed in the 1812 regulations. Like the preceding plate, of the second pattern, the original plate from which this reproduction was made was excavated on the site of Smith's Cantonment at Sackets Harbor, New York. Made of tin-alloy, as is the original, and rectangular with clipped corners, the piece is dominated by an unusually fierce looking eagle that first appeared on one of the 1807 half-dollars struck

13

FIGURE 9

"white metal," the color used by the infantry and dragoons. It is rectangular with clipped corners that are pierced for attachment. No detailed description of the 1812 plate has ever been found, but several identical specimens are known attached to dragoon helments made by a contractor named Henry Cressman. The name "Cressman" is stamped on the lower side of the visor alongside the initials of an inspector named George Flomerfelt, who is known to have been employed by the Army as an inspector in Philadelphia during the period. Henry Cressman is listed in the Philadelphia directories from 1807 through 1817 as a shoemaker. From 1825 to 1839 he is listed as a military cap maker.

FIGURE 10

at the Philadelphia Mint. The eagle has an outsized, curved upper beak and is grasping lightning bolts in the right talon and an olive branch in the left. Below is a panoply of flags and muskets with drum, saber, and cartridge box. The corps designation "US INFAN^Y." is above, and the unit designation "16 REG^T" is below. The "16" appears to have been added with separate die strikes. The specimen is pierced with two pairs of holes on each side for attachment.

This third pattern was also struck in brass and silvered for wear by officers. Several fragments of such a plate were excavated at Sackets Harbor; these, although of the third pattern, are the product of a die different from that used in striking the piece described above.

DRAGOON CAP PLATE, 1812

USNM 62054-M (S-K 1807). Figure 10.

This is an almost exact duplicate of the 1800 dragoon plate except that it is struck in pewter,

¶ On January 12, 1814, Irvine wrote to the Secretary of War as follows: "I send herewith an infantry cap plate which, with your permission, I will substitute for that now in use. The advantages of the former over the latter are that it is lighter, neater, and will not cost half [the] price. The present plate covers the greater part of the front of the cap, is heavy in its

14

FIGURE 11.—Specimen in Campbell collection.

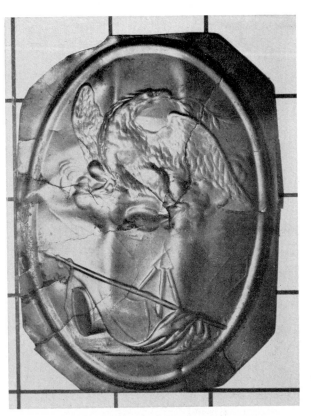

FIGURE 12.—Specimen in Campbell collection.

appearance, and adds much to the weight of the cap . . . .[57] This proposal was approved on January 18.[58]

But here we enter an area of some confusion and controversy. Were these new plates to carry the name of the corps and/or the number of the regiment? Irvine's correspondence gives us no clue, but on the following March 28 he wrote at least two of his deputy commissary generals that he was forwarding 8,752 plates for distribution to 14 specifically named infantry regiments plus 851 "blank" plates.[59] From the total of 8,752 forwarded for specific units, it would seem that these were probably plates of the new design, but then the variance in the number sent for individual regiments—from a low of 152 for the 5th Infantry to highs of 1,016 and 1,050 for the 19th and 25th, respectively—appears odd. Specimens of the 1812 pattern are known both with and without the regimental number, while no examples of the 1814 pattern have been found with unit

[57] Letter in Records AGO.
[58] Letter from Secretary of War to Irvine (Records AGO).
[59] Letters in Records AGO.

designation. Two extant examples of the 1814 pattern, representing two very similar but distinct designs (figs. 11, 12), were excavated at Sackets Harbor, New York, and Fort Atkinson, Nebraska, where Regular infantry served during 1813–1816 and 1819–1821, respectively. Both plates are "blank," and there is no appropriate place on either for the addition of the number of the unit, as in the case of the 1812 pattern.

Another example of the 1814 pattern is known; it is attached to a bell-crowned cap of Militia origin, which indicates that the plate was adopted by the Militia after being discarded by the Regular Establishment. A plate of the same design, but struck in pewter and cut in the diamond shape popular in the 1820's and 1830's, is also known; it is obviously a Militia item.

INFANTRY CAP PLATE, 1814–1821, DIE SAMPLE

USNM 60284–M (S–K 42). Figure 13.

Like practically all die samples, this one is struck in brass. It is rectangular with unclipped corners, but

15

FIGURE 13

infantry officer during the period 1814–1821. The cap is of the style first issued in October 1813, with the front rising above the crown.[61]

The plate, of silver on copper, is rectangular with four scallops top and bottom. A floral border, $\frac{3}{16}$ of an inch wide, that surrounds the whole, strongly suggests that it was an officer's plate. Within a central oval an eagle, with wings outspread, is superimposed upon a trophy of arms and flags; above, on a ribbon, are "E PLURIBUS UNUM" and 15 5-pointed stars. It is possible that this plate is a Militia item, but the fact that it appears to be original on a leather cap of the type worn by Regulars makes it more likely that it is another example of officers' license in the matter of insignia during this period. Its attachment to the cap is a variant method: two hasp-like metal loops, affixed to the plate, have been run through holes in the hat and a leather thong threaded

FIGURE 14

is marked for clipping. Within a raised oval an eagle, very similar to that on the 1812 plate, carries an olive branch in its beak, three arrows in its right talon, and thunder bolts and lightning in its left talon; below, there is a trophy of stacked muskets, drum, flag, and shield. Although this specimen is struck in brass, the plate in used specimens is known only in silver on copper, despite the fact that there was considerable talk of issuing it in brass.[60]

CAP PLATE, INFANTRY OFFICER, 1814–1821

USNM 604747 (S–K 892). Figure 14.

This plate, which is original to the hat to which it is affixed, may well have been worn by a regular

---

[60] Letters in Records AGO: Irvine to James Calhoun (Deputy Commissary General of Purchases, Baltimore), January 14, 1815; Irvine to General Scott, January 13, 1815; Irvine to George Armitage, July 10, 1815.

[61] See McBARRON, "The 18th U.S. Infantry," pp. 48–49.

FIGURE 15.—Specimen in Fort Erie Museum,
Ontario, Canada.

FIGURE 16.—Specimen in Campbell collection.

through them. Most cap plates of this period were pierced at the corners for attachment by threads.

¶ The cap plates issued to the artillery regiments (less the Regiment of Light Artillery) and the riflemen during the period 1812–1821 are known, but only a fragment of one is represented in the national collections. Illustrations of all extant are included to complete the picture. Two of the 1812 plates issued the 2d Regiment of Artillery (fig. 15) have been excavated at Fort Erie, Ontario, and are in the collections of the museum there. A plate of the 3d Regiment (fig. 16) excavated at Sackets Harbor, New York, is of an entirely different design. The lower third of a plate of the 1st Regiment (fig. 17), again of a different design, was excavated by the authors in 1961. In 1814, when the three regiments were consolidated into the Corps of Artillery, these plates were superseded by one bearing the eagle-on-cannon device closely resembling the button of the

artillery for the period 1814–1821, which has the word "Corps" inscribed.[62] Specimens of this latter plate representing two distinct though similar designs have been excavated at posts known to have been manned by Regular artillery in 1814 and later (figs. 18, 19). The same general design appears also on crossbelt plates and waist-belt plates (see below pp. 34–35).

CAP PLATE, 1ST REGIMENT ARTILLERY, 1812

USNM 67240–M. Figure 17.

The over-all design of the plate of which this brass-struck fragment represents approximately one-third can be rather accurately surmised by comparing it with several of the ornamented buttons issued to the infantry in 1812–1815. It is probably the work of the same designer.[63] The plate is rectangular with

---

[62] See JOHNSON, vol. 1, p. 45, and vol. 2, pl. 10.
[63] See JOHNSON, vol. 2, specimen nos. 183, 184, 210–213.

FIGURE 17

FIGURE 18.—Specimen in Campbell collection.

clipped corners. Within a raised border is an oval surrounded by cannon, cannon balls, and a drum, with the unit designation "1 $R^T ART^Y$". At the top of the oval can be seen grasping claws, obviously those of an eagle (as sketched in by the artist) and similar to those on the buttons referred to above. Single holes at the clipped corners provided means of attachment. It seems probable that the design of the missing portion also include flags and additional arms and accoutrements.

¶ The design of the "yellow front plate" authorized and issued to the Regiment of Light Artillery [64] in 1812 was unknown for many years. In May 1961 one of the authors fortunately located this plate (fig. 20) in the collections of the Niagara Historical Society

Museum at Niagara-on-the-Lake, Ontario, included in a group of British badges of the War of 1812 period. There can be no doubt that the specimen is American: the eagle's head is of the same design as that on the third pattern 1812 infantry cap plate (fig. 9); the wreath of laurel appears on both the 1800 and 1812 dragoon helmet plates; and the thunderbolts in the eagle's right talon are wholly American, as opposed to British, and are of the period. In the Fort Ticonderoga Museum collections there is a gold signet ring (original owner unknown) that has an almost identical design.

This is one of the largest plates ever worn by the Regular Establishment. It measures $4\frac{1}{4}$ by $5\frac{3}{4}$ inches, and it is not surprising that it was replaced because of its size. On May 19, 1814, the Commissary General of Purchases wrote Lt. Col. J. R. Fenwick, second-in-command of the light artillery, asking his opinion of a new design and stating flatly: "The present light artillery plate is too large by one-half." [65] The plate illustrated as figure 21 is offered as a pos-

[64] Letter dated February 26, 1812, from Irvine to Secretary of War (Records AGO). In clothing returns for 1812 of light artillery companies stationed at Williamsville, N. Y., "caps and plates" are listed as being "on hand" (Records AGO).

[65] Letter in Records AGO.

FIGURE 19.—Specimen in U.S. Army Artillery and Missile Center Museum, Fort Sill, Oklahoma.

FIGURE 20.—Specimen in Niagara Historical Society Museum, Niagara-on-the-Lake, Ontario, Canada.

FIGURE 21.—Specimen in Campbell collection.

sible example of the 1814 design. A matching waist-belt plate is described below (p. 34).

There are four different patterns of riflemen's cap plates that can be fairly bracketed in three periods. The large (6¼ by 5 inches) diamond-shaped brass plate with the letters "R.R." (fig. 22) was adopted for wear in the spring of 1812 as replacement for the letters "USRR" that had been worn on the cap since the organization of the Regiment of Riflemen in 1808. It was excavated in the interior of one of the barracks comprising Smith's Cantonment at Sackets Harbor, New York, where riflemen were stationed as early as August 1812. The style of the "R" is very similar to that on the 1812 Artillery cap plate, and the "R.R." designation conforms to that on the button authorized for the riflemen in 1808. The pattern of the second diamond-shaped plate (fig. 23), also in brass and almost identical in size, although a ground find, is more difficult to account for, despite the fact that it most certainly falls in the

FIGURE 22.—Specimen in Campbell collection.

FIGURE 23.—Specimen in Campbell collection.

same period. The most logical explanation seems that the riflemen, who considered themselves a cut above the common infantry, became disgruntled with the utter plainness of their plates when compared with those just issued the infantry, and asked for and received, possibly late in 1812, the plate with the eagle and the designation "U.S. Rifle Men." The fact that the plate bears the designation "1 REGᵀ"— although there were no other rifle regiments from 1812 to 1814—can be explained by reference to the "national color" of the Rifle Regiment completed in 1808, which bore the inscription "1st Rifle Regt.— U.S." and the standard and national color of the light artillery which were inscribed "The First Regiment of Light Artillery" when there was never more than one light artillery unit in the Army.[66] In any case, accurate dating of the third and fourth patterns definitely places the second pattern in the 1812–1813 period by process of elimination. It was superseded in 1814[67] very possibly for the same reason that the infantry plate was changed—heaviness in both appearance and weight—and replaced by a

plate with a "design similar to that of the button . . . flat yellow buttons which shall exhibit a bugle surrounded by stars with the number of the regiment within the curve of the bugle."[68] At least three specimens of this third-pattern plate are known. They all are 3¼ inches in diameter, and thus are large enough for a hat frontpiece and too large to be a cockade device. One of these plates is without a numeral (fig. 24); one has the numeral "1," and one has the numeral "4" (fig. 25). The first and second of these were found at Fort Atkinson, but very probably were not worn as late as 1819–1821. Portions of specimens of this 1814 plate have also been recovered from an early Pawnee village site in Webster County, Nebraska, indicating their possible use as trade goods after the rifle regiment changed its plates in 1817.[69] The fourth pattern, with an eagle over a horn (fig. 26) was authorized[70] in 1817.

[68] Letter dated January 12, 1814, from Irvine to Secretary of War (Records AGO).

[69] See KIVETT, p. 59.

[70] A letter dated July 29, 1817, from Irvine to Secretary of War describes the device; a letter dated August 4, 1817, from the Adjutant and Inspector General (Daniel Parker) to Irvine authorizes the plate but gives no description. Both letters are in Records AGO.

[66] See KUHN, pp. 263–267, and DAVIS, pp. 13–14 and pl. 3.
[67] Act of February 10, 1814 (*Military Laws*, pp. 251–252).

20

FIGURE 24.—Specimen in Campbell collection.

FIGURE 26.—Specimen in Campbell collection.

FIGURE 25

Apparently it was worn until 1821, since several examples of it have been found at Atkinson; other examples also are known.

The cap plate for the U.S. Military Academy, c. 1815, is illustrated (fig. 27) because it completes the cycle for insignia of the Regular Establishment for the period. Apparently it is the work of the same designer as most of the insignia of the period 1812–

FIGURE 27.—Specimen in collection of Waverly P. Lewis, Devon, Connecticut.

1815. Scratched on its reverse side is the name George W. Frost, a Virginian who entered the Military Academy as a cadet in 1814 and resigned on March 8, 1816.

The two plates of the U.S. Marine Corps, despite the fact that they are naval rather than military, are included because they fit very precisely into the device design pattern of the strictly army items of the period and because they are unique in their rarity.

CAP PLATE, U.S. MARINE CORPS, C. 1807, DIE SAMPLE

USNM 58671–N–(1). Figure 28.

This specimen was extremely puzzling for many years. The design is obviously that of the War of 1812 period, bearing strong similarity to both the 1812 and 1814 infantry plates and the 1814 Artillery Corps plate, possibly the work of the same die sinker. The 1804 Marine Corps uniform regulations specified merely a "Brass Eagle and Plate," but the 1807 regulations called for "Octagon plates." [71] Thus there was considerable reluctance to accept this die sample as the authentic design. In the summer of

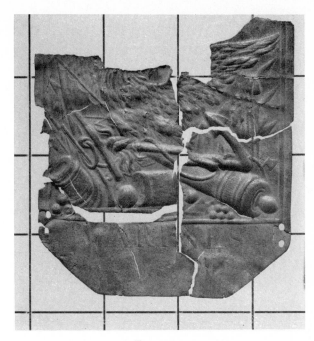

FIGURE 29

1959, however, the authors, excavating at Fort Tomkins, New York, which was known to have had a small barracks for the use of naval personnel ashore, recovered parts of two brass plates of this identical design, and in the octagon shape—that is, retangular with clipped corners (fig. 29). The design may thus be precisely dated.

The specimen is struck in rectangular brass with a raised edge. The whole is dominated by an eagle that is very similar to the eagles on the infantry and artillery corps plates described above. The talons grasp the shank of a large fouled anchor; a ribbon, held in the beak and streaming overhead, is embossed with the motto "FORTITUDINE." The whole is on a trophy of arms and flags, and below the lower raised edge is embossed the word "MARINES." The excavated specimens vary slightly in size, but average $3\frac{3}{8}$ by $4\frac{3}{4}$ inches. Reproductions of this die strike were made prior to its acquisition by the National Museum, and specimens outside the national collections should be considered with caution.

CAP OR SHOULDER-BELT PLATE, U.S. MARINE CORPS, 1815–1825(?)

USNM 58671–N–(2). Figure 30.

This specimen is known only in die samples. Because of its similarity in design to the 1814 infantry

FIGURE 28

---

[71] See MCCLELLAN, pp. 25, 44.

FIGURE 30

plates, it cannot be dated later than 1825. Since no naval uniformed Militia units are known for the period 1815–1825, and since the plate is obviously not a device of the regular Navy, it must be assigned to the Marine Corps. In studying this plate, however, we must recognize the possibility that the maker may have been designing and sinking dies in the hope of having a sample accepted and approved for issue rather than actually executing a contract. The plate is struck in rectangular brass, and the corners are marked for clipping. The design, within a wide oval with raised edge, consists of an eagle above a trophy of arms, flags, and a shield. The right talon grasps a fluke of a fouled anchor, and the left talon holds the pike of a stand of colors. Reproductions of this die strike were made prior to its acquisition by the National Museum, and specimens outside the national collections should be considered with caution.

¶ The 1821 uniform regulations were significant in several respects: cap plates were eliminated as distinctive insignia of the various arms; the color of certain items of dress and equipment remained the sole distinction; and the rules regarding nonregulation dress were more precisely stated than before. The cap plates were replaced by eagles, measuring 3

inches between wing tips, and the number of the regiment was cut in the shield. Regulations tersely stated that "all articles of uniform or equipment, more or less, than those prescribed, or in any manner differing from them, are prohibited."[72] General and staff officers were to wear black sword belts with "yellow plates"; artillery officers were to wear white waist belts with a yellow oval plate 1½ inches wide and with an eagle in the center; infantry officers were to wear a similar plate that was white instead of yellow. Cockade eagles for *chapeau de bras* were to be gold and measure 1½ inches between wing tips. Since enlisted men were no longer authorized to wear swords, they had no waist belts.

CAP AND PLATE, THIRD ARTILLERY, 1821

USNM 66603–M. Figure 31.

Although several "yellow" eagles that can be attributed to the 1821–1832 period are known, this brass specimen on the bell-crowned cap is the only one known to the authors that has the prescribed regimental number cut out of the shield. The button on the pompon rosette—which appears to be definitely original to the cap, as does the eagle—carries the artillery "A," thus the assignment to that branch of

FIGURE 31

[72] *General Regulations*, pp. 154–162.

23

the service. The eagle bears a close similarity to the eagles on the 1812 and 1814 infantry cap plates and the 1807 Marine Corps cap plate, and is possibly the work of the same designer.

CAP INSIGNIA, INFANTRY, 1822

USNM 60364–M (SK–120). Figure 32.

Early in 1822, the Secretary of War, acting on a suggestion of Callendar Irvine, ordered that all metal equipment of the infantry be of "white metal" in keeping with its pompons, tassels, and lace.[73] This specimen, struck in copper and silvered, is believed to have been issued as a result of that order.

¶ The 1821 regulations stated that cockade eagles should measure 1½ inches between wing tips. In 1832 this wingspread was increased to 2½ inches. Thus, specimens of a relatively uniform pattern and measuring approximately 1½ inches in wingspread will be considered as of the Regular Army, 1821–1832. Similarly, those of a relatively uniform pattern and measuring approximately 2½ inches in wingspread are dated 1832–1851.

COCKADE EAGLE, C. 1821

USNM 60371–M (S–K 127). Figure 33.

This eagle, struck in brass, has wings extended, head to the right, federal shield on breast with no stars, olive branch in right talon, and three arrows in left talon.

FIGURE 32

---

[73] Letter dated January 4, 1822, from Secretary of War to Irvine (Records AGO).

FIGURE 33

COCKADE EAGLE, INFANTRY, C. 1821

USNM 60372–M (S–K 128). Not illustrated.

This eagle is struck from the same die as the preceding specimen, but it is in white metal rather than brass.

COCKADE EAGLE, C. 1821

USNM 60367–M (S–K 123). Figure 34.

Of silver on copper, this eagle is similar to the two preceding specimens, but is struck from a variant die. It possibly was worn by the Militia.

COCKADE EAGLE, INFANTRY, C. 1821

USNM 60373–M (S–K 130). Figure 35.

This specimen is very similar to those above, but it has 13 stars in the shield on the eagle's breast.

¶ Despite the fact that it was found attached to a shako of distinct Militia origin, the cap plate shown in figure 36 is believed to be that prescribed for the cadets of the Military Academy in the 1821 uniform regulations and described as "yellow plate, diamond shape." The letters "U S M A" in the angles of the diamond, the word "CADET" at the top of the oval, what appears to be the designation "W POINT" at the left top of the map, and the tools of instruction (so similar to those embellishing the cadet diploma,

FIGURE 34

FIGURE 36.—Specimen in West Point Museum, West Point, New York.

although totally different in rendering), make it difficult to assign this plate to any source other than the Academy. It is possible, of course, that this was a manufacturer's sample which was never actually adopted for wear at West Point. The apparent maker's name, "CASAD," at the bottom of the oval, does not appear in the city directories of any of the larger manufacturing centers of the period.

CAP INSIGNIA, 1832 (?)

USNM 60365–M (S–K 121). Figure 37.

Despite the facts that there was no change in cap insignia authorized in the 1832 uniform regulations and that this specimen is similar in most respects to

FIGURE 35

FIGURE 37

the 1821 eagle, its refinement of design and manufacture indicates that it possibly belongs to the period of the 1830's and 1840's. It is struck in thin brass and has three plain wire fasteners soldered to the reverse.

CAP INSIGNIA, 1832(?)

USNM 60366-M (S-K 122). Not illustrated.

Although similar to the preceding plate, this specimen measures 3¼ by 2¼ inches, is struck from a different die, and has a much wider breast shield. Of somewhat heavier brass than most such similar eagles and exhibiting a well-developed patina, it may have been an officer's device.

CAP PLATE, DRAGOONS, 1833

USNM 60276-M (S-K 34). Figure 38.

When the dragoons returned to the Army in 1833, their cap device was described as "a gilt star, silver eagle . . . the star to be worn in front." [74] An 8-pointed, sunburst-type star, this plate is struck in brass and has a superimposed eagle that is struck in brass and silvered. The eagle is basically the Napoleonic type adopted by the British after the Battle of

FIGURE 38

[74] General Order No. 38, Headquarters of the Army, May 2, 1833. (Photostatic copy in files of division of military history, Smithsonian Institution.)

Waterloo and altered by omitting the lightning in the talons and adding a wreath to the breast. Plain wire fasteners are soldered to the back.

¶ In 1834, possibly as a result of the newly organized dragoons receiving distinctive branch insignia, the infantry and artillery once again were authorized devices on the dress cap designating their particular arm. The gilt eagle was retained. Below the eagle was an open horn with cords and tassels in silver for infantry, and cross cannons in "gilt" for artillery. The number of the regiment was added over the cannon or within the curve of the horn. These devices remained in use until the change in headgear in 1851.

CAP INSIGNIA, INFANTRY, 1834–1851

USNM 62055-M, 62056-M (SK-1808, 1809). Figure 39.

This eagle is similar to the 1821 pattern, although somewhat more compact in design. It is struck in brass, has wings upraised, head to the right, shield on breast, olive branch in right talon, and three arrows in left talon. The open horn, struck in brass and silvered, is suspended, with bell to the right, by four twisted cords tied in a 3-leaf-clover knot; the tassels on the four cord-ends hang below.

CAP INSIGNIA, ARTILLERY, 1834–1851

USNM 60426-M (S-K 182). Figure 40.

This is the "gilt . . . cross cannons" device prescribed for artillery in the 1834 regulations. Struck in sheet brass of medium thickness, the superimposed cannon has trunions and dolphins.

FORAGE CAP STAR, DRAGOON OFFICER, C. 1840

USNM 604967-M (S-K 1111). Figure 41.

Although uniform regulations for the period of the 1830's and 1840's make no mention of a distinctive device for the dragoon forage cap, photographs in the National Archives show that officers' caps, at least, carried a 6-pointed star, apparently gold-embroidered.[75] This specimen is believed to be such a star. Made of gold bullion and with rather large sequins sewed onto a heavy paper background, the star is mounted on dark blue wool. The

[75] TOWNSEND AND TODD, pp. 1–2.

FIGURE 39

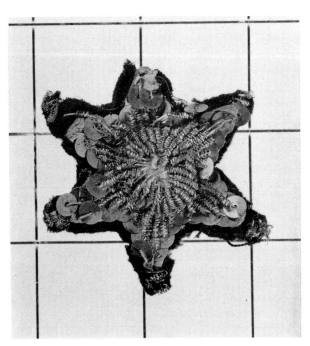

FIGURE 41

points of the star are extended with gold embroidery on the cloth.

CAP INSIGNIA, CADETS, U.S. MILITARY ACADEMY, 1842, AND ENGINEER SOLDIERS, 1846

USNM 604529 (S–K 676). Figure 42.

In 1839 the cadets at the Military Academy discarded the bell-crowned caps they had worn since 1821 and wore a cylindrical black shako similar to that worn by the Regular artillery and infantry. The

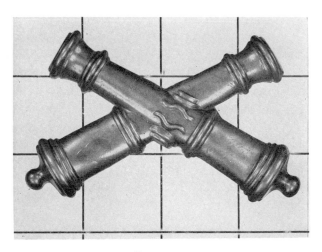

FIGURE 40

FIGURE 42

artillery gilt eagle and crossed cannon replaced the diamond-shaped plate on the front. In 1842–1843 the crossed cannon were replaced by the engineer castle as more in keeping with the original mission of the Academy and the general orientation of its curriculum.

Shortly after the beginning of hostilities with Mexico in 1846, the Congress authorized the enlistment of a company of "engineer soldiers" that was designated the Company of Sappers, Miners, and Pontoniers. These were the first enlisted men authorized the Corps of Engineers since the period of the War of 1812. The headgear for these men was prescribed as "Schako—same pattern as that of the artillery, bearing a yellow eagle over a castle like that worn by the Cadets."[76]

Struck in thin to medium brass, this plate is the familiar turreted castle of the Corps of Engineers so well known today. It was worn below the eagle.

¶ To complete the branches of the Regular Establishment during the Mexican War period, the Regiment of Voltigeurs and Foot Riflemen must be mentioned, although they were apparently without any distinctive branch insignia.

The regiment was constituted on February 11, 1847, and its uniform [77] was prescribed 9 days later in the War Department's General Order No. 7. However, the regiment was issued infantry woolen jackets and trousers and never received what little gray issue clothing was sent to them in Mexico almost a year later. Uniform trimmings were to be as for the infantry, with the substitution of the letter "v" where appropriate. So far as presently known, this substitution affected only the button pattern—an appropriate letter "v" on the shield centered on the eagle's breast.

The 1851 uniform regulations radically changed almost every item of the Army's dress. Most of the distinctive devices were also altered, although more in size and composition than general design. Some devices were completely eliminated. While officers retained insignia of their arm or branch on their hats, enlisted personnel, with the exception of those of engineers and ordnance, had only the letter of their company, their particular arm being designated by the color of collars, cuffs, bands on hats, pompons,

epaulets, chevrons, and the like. A newly designed sword or waist-belt plate was prescribed for all personnel. All items of uniform and insignia authorized in 1851 were included in an illustrated edition of the *Regulations for the Uniform and Dress of the Army of the United States, June 1851,* published by William H. Horstmann and Sons, well-known uniform and insignia dealers in Philadelphia.[78]

POMPON EAGLE, 1851

USNM 604853 (S–K 998). Figure 43.

Worn attached to the base of the pompon by all enlisted personnel, this brass eagle, similar in general design to that worn on the shako in the 1830's, stands with wings upraised, olive branch in right talon, three arrows in left talon, and a scroll, with national motto, in beak. Above are stars, clouds, and bursts of sun rays. Officers wore an eagle of similar design of gold embroidery on cloth.

CAP INSIGNIA, GENERAL AND STAFF OFFICERS, 1851

USNM 604862 (S–K 1007). Figure 44.

This specimen, in accord with regulations, is on dark blue cloth and consists of a gold-embroidered wreath encircling Old English letters "u.s." in silver bullion. Embroidered insignia of this period were all made by hand, and they varied considerably in both detail and size. During the 1861–1865 period the same design was made about half this size for wear on officers' forage caps, and the device appeared in variant forms. One example is known where the numeral "15" is embroidered over the letters "u.s.";[79] and Miller's *Photographic History of the Civil War* includes several photos of general officers whose wreath insignia on the forage cap substitute small rank insignia stars for the letters.

CAP INSIGNIA, OFFICER, ENGINEERS, 1851

USNM 300720. Figure 45.

On dark blue cloth, this device comprises a gold-embroidered wreath of laurel and palm encircling a turreted castle in silver metal as prescribed in regu-

---

[76] *General Regulations for the Army of the United States, 1847,* pp. 192–193.

[77] A detailed description is given in *Military Collector and Historian* (June 1952), vol. 4, no. 2, p. 44.

[78] A partial republication of this work appears in *Military Collector and Historian,* vol. 10, no. 1 (spring 1958), pp. 16, 17; no. 2 (summer 1958), pp. 43–45.

[79] LEWIS, p. 64.

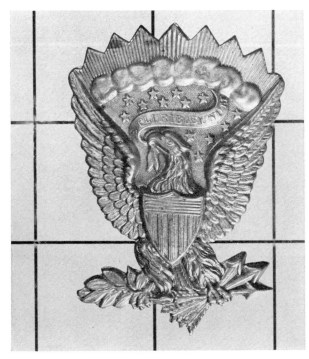

FIGURE 43

FIGURE 45

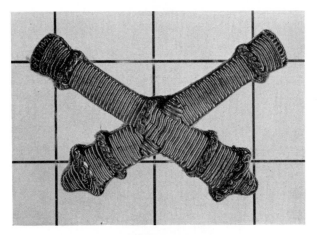

FIGURE 46

lations. Other examples are known with the castle embroidered.

HAT INSIGNIA, OFFICER, ARTILLERY, 1851

USNM 604872 (S–K 1017).   Figure 46.

This specimen adheres almost exactly to the 1851 regulations, but it lacks the number of the regiment as called for. The number was a separate insignia

embroidered above the cannon. The cannon are of gold embroidery. The device was also made in gold metal imitation-embroidery in several variant designs.

CAP INSIGNIA, OFFICER, INFANTRY, 1851

USNM 604888 (S–K 1033).   Figure 47.

On dark blue cloth, this device is the well-known looped horn in gold embroidery with three cords and tassels. The regimental number "4," in silver bullion, lies within the loop of the horn. This insignia is also common in metal imitation-embroidery.

CAP AND COLLAR INSIGNIA, ENLISTED ORDNANCE, 1851

USNM 604520 (S–K 667).   Figure 48.

Struck in brass, this device was worn on the caps and coat collars of ordnance enlisted personnel. Although the shell and flame insignia appears in a

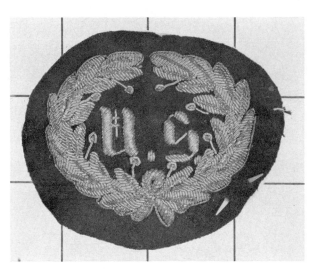

FIGURE 44

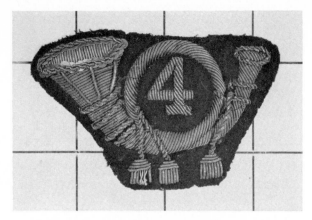

FIGURE 47

FIGURE 49

FIGURE 48

and drawing in the Horstmann publication of the regulations.

CAP INSIGNIA, DRAGOON OFFICERS, 1851

USNM 604879 (S–K 1024).   *Figure 50.*

Comprising crossed sabers of gold, with edges upward, this insignia is similar to the well-known device worn by the Regular cavalry as late as 1953.

¶ In 1846 the Regiment of Mounted Riflemen was organized to consolidate the northern route to the Pacific by establishing and manning a series of posts along the Oregon Trail.[80] The outbreak of the War with Mexico postponed this mission and the unit was diverted to the theater of operations. Shortly after the regiment was constituted it was authorized

number of variations of design, this specimen conforms exactly to the regulations of 1851 as published by Horstmann.

CAP AND COLLAR INSIGNIA, ENGINEER SOLDIERS, 1851

USNM 61618.   *Figure 49.*

The 1851 uniform regulations called for a "castle of yellow metal one and five-eighths inches by one and one-fourth inches high" on both the coat collar and the hat of "Engineer Soldiers." This specimen, struck in brass, conforms exactly to the descriptions

FIGURE 50

[80]Act of May 19, 1846 (*Military Laws*, pp. 371–372).

to wear a forage cap device prescribed as "a gold embroidered spread eagle, with the letter R in silver, on the shield."[81] No surviving specimen of this insignia is known, and there seems some doubt that it was ever actually manufactured.[82]

CAP INSIGNIA, OFFICER, REGIMENT OF MOUNTED RIFLEMEN, 1850

USNM 604854 (SK 999). Figure 51.

In 1850 the regiment was given a "trumpet" hat device. Officers were to wear "a trumpet, perpendicular, embroidered in gold, with the number of the regiment, in silver, within the bend."[83] This trumpet is also known in metal imitation-embroidery. The prescribed regimental number, which is illustrated in the Horstmann publication of the regulations (pl. 15), is not included on the device, probably because there was but one such unit in the Regular Establishment.

CAP INSIGNIA, ENLISTED, REGIMENT OF MOUNTED RIFLEMEN, 1850

USNM 62053–M (SK–1806). Figure 52.

The same general order that gave rifle officers a gold-embroidered trumpet prescribed for enlisted men a similar device to be of "yellow metal." This insignia lasted but one year for the men in the ranks, being unmentioned in the 1851 regulations.

Shoulder-Belt and Waist-Belt Plates

Oval shoulder-belt plates were worn by American officers during the War of the Revolution, but no extant specimens are known. Highly ornamented or engraved officers' plates for the period after 1790 are in several collections (fig. 53) and others are illustrated in contemporary portraits (fig. 54). Just what year shoulder-belt plates were issued to enlisted personnel is unknown, but their use appears to have been well established by 1812. The uniform regulations for

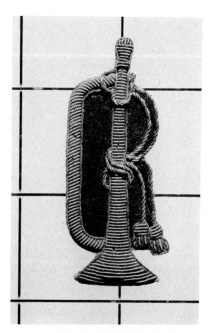

FIGURE 51

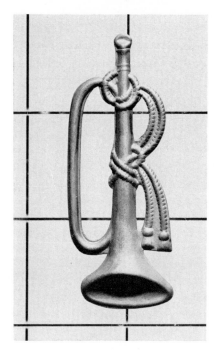

FIGURE 52

that year specified swords for sergeants of infantry to be "worn with a white cross belt 3½ inches wide," but nothing was said about a device on the belt.[84]

---

[81] General Order No. 18, June 4, 1846, War Department (photostatic copy in files of division of military history, Smithsonian Institution).

[82] Insignia of the riflemen are discussed by TOWNSEND AND TODD, pp. 2–3.

[83] General Order No. 2, February 13, 1850, War Department (photostatic copy in files of division of military history, Smithsonian Institution).

---

[84] General Order, Southern Department U.S. Army, January 24, 1813 (photostatic copy in files of division of military history, Smithsonian Institution).

FIGURE 53.—Specimen in Campbell collection.

FIGURE 54.—Portrait in collection of The
Filson Club, Louisville, Kentucky.

Normally, brass or "yellow metal" plates were
authorized for the artillery and silvered or "white
metal" for the infantry and dragoons, as consonant
with the rest of their trimmings. In actuality, however, white-metal shoulder-belt plates do not seem to
have been issued to the infantry prior to 1814, and
brass ones were still being issued in 1815.[85] Most of
these plates were plain oval, although a few are known
that were struck with devices similar to those on cap
plates; and at least one rectangular cap plate, fitted
with the two studs and hook on the reverse normal to
shoulder-belt plates, has been found. It seems
probable that these were officers' plates. Oval brass
plates have been found that are identical in size and
construction to the plain ones but with the letters
"U.S." embossed on them; however, these are difficult
to date.

It is extremely doubtful that waist-belt plates were
issued to enlisted personnel of foot units during this
period. In 1808 enlisted dragoons were authorized

a waist-belt plate of tinned brass and, as far as known,
perfectly plain.[86]

The 1812 regulations prescribed for the light dragoons a "buff leather waist belt, white plate in front
with eagle in relief," and there is the possibility that
the light artillery had such. In actuality, there was
no call for a waist belt where a shoulder belt was
authorized. Neither civilian trousers nor the few
surviving military "pantaloons" of the period are
fitted with belt loops, trousers being held up either
by suspenders or by being buttoned directly to the
shirt or waistcoat. No example of the dragoon plate
has been found. However, a rather tantalizing possibility exists—a fragment of a pewter belt plate
(fig. 55) was excavated at Sackets Harbor, New York,
where the light dragoons are known to have served.
The 1816 regulations specified for artillerymen
"waist belts of white leather two inches wide, yellow oval plate of the same width." It is not made
clear, however, whether this belt and plate was for

[85] Letters from Irvine in Records AGO: To Colonel Bogardus (Commanding Officer, 41st Infantry), February 16, 1814;
to James Calhoun, January 14, 1815; and to General Scott,
January 31, 1815.

[86] Letter to the Purveyor of Public Supplies in 1808.

32

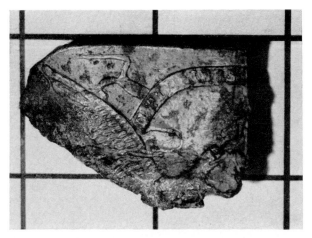

FIGURE 55.—Specimen in Campbell collection.

FIGURE 56.—Specimen in Campbell collection.

FIGURE 57

officers only or for all ranks. The unusually striking oval specimen (fig. 56) may be this plate, but its ornateness indicates that this particular design was for officers only.

SHOULDER-BELT PLATE, 1790(?)–1812

USNM 12804. Figure 57.

This plate was worn by Peter Gansevoort sometime during his military career, probably after 1790. Gansevoort, between 1775 and his death in 1812, was successively major, lieutenant colonel, colonel, and brigadier general of New York State Militia and brigadier general U.S. Army (1809–1812). Although distinctly Militia in design, the specimen is included here as an example of the wide variety of such devices worn by officers of the 1800–1821 period.

This plate is octagonal, slightly convex, and has beveled edges. The design is hand engraved on cop-

per, and the whole is gold plated. Within an engraved border is the eagle-on-half-globe device of New York State. Two studs and a hook soldered to the reverse are not believed to be original.

SHOULDER-BELT PLATE, INFANTRY OFFICER, C. 1812

USNM 604313 (S–K 469). Figure 58.

This rectangular, slightly convex plate of silver on copper has beveled edges and a small slot in the center for the attachment of an ornament. The ornament is missing, although it can be surmised that it was an eagle. The reverse is fitted with two studs and a hook and bears the hallmark of "W. Pinchin, Philad ª." William Pinchin is listed in the Philadelphia directory for 1809 as a silversmith at 326 Sassafras Street. The 1810 directory lists only "Widow of," but another William Pinchin (probably the son) appears in the 1820's.

WAIST-BELT PLATE, LIGHT ARTILLERY(?), 1814–1821

USNM 60452–M (S–K 208). Figure 59.

The design of this rectangular plate, struck in rather heavy brass, is the same as that offered as the

33

FIGURE 58

FIGURE 60

1814-pattern cap plate for the light artillery, although it is the product of a different and somewhat more crudely sunk die. The piece is dominated by an eagle with wings upraised, a shield on its breast, three arrows in its right talon, and an olive branch in its left talon. Crossed cannon are in the foreground, and there is a pile of six cannon balls in the lower right corner. The whole is superimposed on a trophy of colors and bayoneted muskets. Above is a 5-pointed "star of stars" made up of 20 5-pointed stars.

FIGURE 59

WAIST-BELT PLATE, OFFICER, ARTILLERY CORPS, 1814–1821

USNM 60448–M (S–K 204). Figure 60.

The rectangular plate is struck in brass on a die of the same design as that used in making the 1814 Artillery Corps cap plate, type I (p. 18). Before the strike was made, a piece of thin sheet iron, slightly narrower than the finished product, was applied to the reverse of the brass. After the strike, which shows through clearly on the iron, the ends of this applied metal were bent inward into tongues for attachments to the belt, and the remainder of the back was filled with pewter. The edges of the obverse were then beveled to finish the product. It seems very probable that plates such as this were produced for sale to officers.

SHOULDER-BELT PLATE, OFFICER, ARTILLERY CORPS, 1814–1821

USNM 60247 (S–K 5). Figure 61.

This is a companion piece to the Artillery Corps waist-belt plate described above. It was struck in brass from the die of the 1814 Artillery Corps cap plate, type I, again with a thin sheet of iron applied to the reverse before the strike. There is no pewter filling; the beveled edges of the piece together with the adhesive effect of the strike—which shows through very clearly—holds on the back. The plate is fitted with two simple bent-wire fasteners for attachment, indicating that it was intended for ornamental use only. Like its waist-belt plate counterpart, this specimen must be considered an officer's device.

34

FIGURE 61

FIGURE 62

SHOULDER-BELT PLATE, INFANTRY, 1814–1821

USNM 60248–M (S–K 6). *Figure 62.*

This specimen is of the same design as the 1814 Infantry cap plate, type I (p. 15). It is oval, with raised edge. Within the oval is an eagle with an olive branch in its beak, three arrows in its right talon, and thunder bolts and lightning in its left talon. Below is a trophy of stacked muskets, drum, flag, and shield. The plate is silver on copper, with sheet-iron backing and bent-wire fasteners. As in the case of the Artillery Corps plate, just preceding, this must be considered an officer's plate. A similar oval plate bearing the design of the 1812 dragoon cap plate, and of similar construction, is known.

SHOULDER-BELT PLATE, 1814

USNM 66478–M. Figures 63, 64.

Excavated on the site of Smith's Cantonment at Sackets Harbor, New York, this plate is interesting in that it differs in both construction and method of

attachment from similar plates of the same period in the national collections. Rather than being struck in thin brass with a backing and fasteners applied to the reverse, this specimen is cast in brass and the edges rather unevenly beveled, with two studs and a narrow tongue for attachment cast integrally with the plate and with hexagonal heads forced over the ends of the studs. This means of attachment, which indicates that the plate was intended to be utilitarian as well as merely ornamental, is similar to that on British plates of the period between the Revolution and the War of 1812. The plate could have been worn by either infantry or artillery, for both were issued brass plates during this period,[87] however, it is more probable that it was worn by the infantry, since the majority of the artillery in the Sackets Harbor area were stationed nearby at either Fort Pike or Fort Tomkins.

---

[87] Letters from Irvine in Records AGO: To Colonel Bogardus, February 16, 1814; to James Calhoun, January 14, 1815.

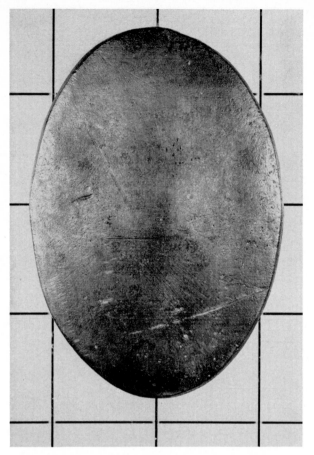

FIGURE 63

SHOULDER-BELT PLATE, C. 1812

USNM 604311 (S–K 467). Figure 65.

The plain, oval, slightly convex plate of brass has a raised edge. The face is lapped over a piece of sheet-iron backing. On the reverse is soldered an early form of bent-wire fasteners. British shoulder-belt plates of the Revolutionary period normally had fasteners cast as integral parts of the plate proper.

SHOULDER-BELT PLATE, C. 1812

USNM 604312 (S–K 468). Not illustrated.

This plate is identical to the one described immediately above except that it is struck in copper and the surface is silvered.

SHOULDER-BELT PLATE, C. 1812

USNM 604314 (S–K 470). Not illustrated.

This plate, struck from solid brass, has a slightly beveled edge and bent-wire fasteners. It is slightly convex. Since it is smaller than the two preceding plates, it could have been designed for the Militia.

SHOULDER-BELT PLATE, 1815(?)–1821

USNM 60399–M (S–K 155). Figure 66.

The two specimens of this plate in the national collections are undocumented. Similar in size and construction to the plain oval brass and silvered plates, it has the raised letters "u.s.," three-fourths inch high in the center. Definitely not later than 1832, it may well have been issued soon after the end of the War of 1812. It is considered a Regular Army item since the Militia did not use the designation "u.s." at this early period. In this latter connection it is interesting to note that an example of the 1812 Infantry cap plate, type II, with the letters "us" crudely stamped out, is known attached to a cap of distinct Militia origin.

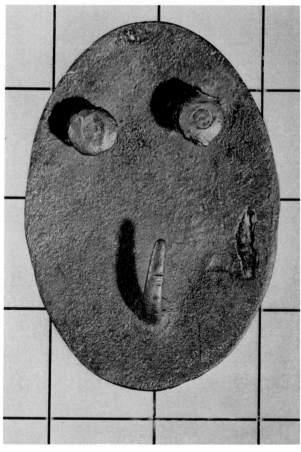

FIGURE 64

36

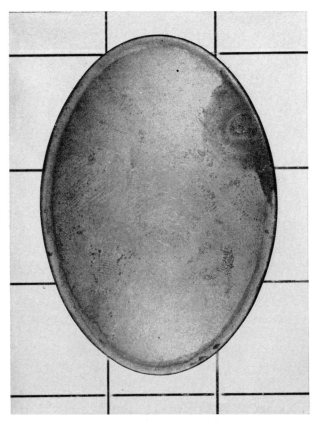

FIGURE 65

FIGURE 66

WAIST-BELT PLATE, GENERAL OFFICER, C. 1816

USNM 38212. Figure 67.

After the War of 1812, the State of New York presented swords to several prominent officers of the Army and Navy who had distinguished themselves in actions within New York or near its borders. One of these swords (USNM 10294) [88] and an unusually fine gold embroidered belt (USNM 33097) with this gold belt buckle were presented to Maj. Gen. Jacob Brown.

Chased in very fine gold, the buckle is considered by experts in the goldsmithing and silversmithing fields to be one of the outstanding pieces of American craftsmanship of its kind. [89] The central motif is the New York State eagle-on-half-globe device on a wreath of the colors. The head of the eagle is very similar to that on the cap plates of the 1807 Marine

FIGURE 67

Corps, 1812 infantry, and 1814 Artillery Corps. The border is of a rose pattern distinctly American in feeling, and in each corner within the border are

---

[88] Detailed descriptions of this sword are given by HAROLD L. PETERSON, pp. 193–194, and BELOTE, pp. 30–31.

[89] Mr. Michael Arpad, well known and highly regarded silversmith, of Washington, D.C., has called this specimen "an exquisite piece of work by a master craftsman."

acanthus leaves in unusually delicate Viennese baroque design.

The maker of this buckle is unknown, but since it is reasonably certain that the hilt of the sword was designed by Moritz Furst (see p. 12), it is possible that the design of the buckle is his also, especially in view of the Viennese touch in the acanthus leaves, his training at the mint in Vienna, and the probability that he designed the 1812 infantry cap plate.

¶ Although the 1821 regulations were very specific about the prohibition of nonregulation items of uniform and equipment, they were somewhat vague regarding specifications. General staff and engineer officers were to wear black belts with a "yellow plate," artillery "yellow oval plates . . . with an eagle in the center," and infantry the same but "white" instead of yellow.[90] No oval plates meeting these vague descriptions are known, but the specimens described below may well have been those actually approved by the Ordnance Department, and thus, worn.

WAIST-BELT PLATE, INFANTRY OFFICER, C. 1822

USNM 604118–M (S–K 274). Figure 68.

This plate, struck in copper and silvered, is round with an outer ring. It is attached to a white buff belt. The plate proper contains an eagle with wings outspread, shield on breast, olive branch in right talon,

and three arrows in left talon. The whole is within a ring of 24 5-pointed stars. The outer ring is decorated as a wreath, and the narrow rectangular belt attachments are embossed with a floral pattern. The 24 stars place this specimen between 1822 and 1836. Similar buckles are known in yellow metal for either staff or artillery and containing 24, 26, and 28 stars, indicating that they probably were worn until the rectangular eagle-wreath plate was prescribed in 1851.

WAIST-BELT PLATE, INFANTRY OFFICER, 1821–1835

USNM 60454 (S–K 210). Figure 69.

This specimen is offered as another possibility for the 1821 regulation plate. It is identical in size and similar in design to the preceding plate. The plate proper contains an eagle with wings spread, a breast shield containing the letter "I," an olive branch in right talon, and three arrows in left talon. There is no outer ring of stars. The outer ring of the buckle is decorated with a wreath, but the rectangular belt attachments are plain. The 1821 regulations called for eagle buttons of "yellow" and "white" metal with the letters "A" and "I" (for artillery and infantry) on the eagle's shield, and the belt plate may have been designed to conform. There is also the possibility that this plate, as well as the one described below, was designed to conform to the 1835 regulations which prescribed a waist belt with a "round" clasp.[91]

FIGURE 68

FIGURE 69

[90] *General Regulations for the Army,* pp. 154–162.

[91] *General Regulations for the Army of the United States,* p. 222.

WAIST-BELT PLATE, ARTILLERY OFFICER, 1821–1835

USNM 60455–M (S–K 211). Not illustrated.

Nearly identical to the infantry officer's plate above, this buckle, in brass, has the artillery "A" on the eagle's breast shield.

¶ Although the regulations for this period do not mention shoulder-belt plates for enlisted men (officers had none as they wore their swords on their waist belts), it can be assumed that they were worn. The two specimens described below must be dated later than 1812–1821 because of the belt attachments. The earlier specimens had rudimentary bent-wire fasteners, but these, more refined, have two round studs and a hook soldered to the plate proper.

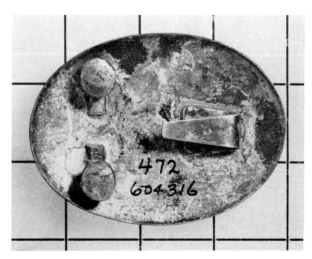

FIGURE 71

SHOULDER-BELT PLATE, INFANTRY, C. 1821

USNM 604316 (S–K 472). Figures 70, 71.

This plate, of silver on copper, is plain oval and slightly convex.

FIGURE 70

SHOULDER-BELT PLATE, ARTILLERY, C. 1821

USNM 604315 (S–K 471). Not illustrated.

This specimen is identical to the preceding one except that it is in plain brass.

¶ The 1832 uniform regulations brought some well-defined changes. General and staff officers were to wear gilt waist-belt plates "having the letters U s and a sprig of laurel on each side in silver," and the bottom of the skirts of officers' coats were to bear

distinctive devices—a gold-embroidered star for general officers and officers of the general staff, a shell and flame in gold embroidery for artillery officers, and silver-embroidered bugles for infantry officers.

WAIST-BELT PLATE, GENERAL AND STAFF OFFICERS, 1832

USNM 664. Figure 72.

The plate and the belt to which it is attached formerly belonged to Capt. Charles O. Collins, an 1824 graduate of the Military Academy. The belt is of patent leather, as specified for undress wear, and is 1½ inches wide. The plate is cast in brass and has raised edges. Rather than having "a sprig of laurel on each side," it has a wreath of laurel enclosing the letters "U s," in Old English, in silvered metal

FIGURE 72

affixed to the front. It is attached on the right side by a rectangular belt attachment with a flat hook on the left rear.

¶ The 1832 regulations specified for engineer officers a waist-belt plate to be "gilt, eliptical, two inches in the shortest diameter, bearing the device of the button." Such a plate (fig. 73) is in the collections of the Valley Forge Chapel Museum. It is entirely possible that this plate is even earlier than 1832, for the 1821 and 1825 regulations state that the engineer buttons were to contain "the device and motto heretofore established."

FIGURE 73

In the collections of the West Point Museum is a button, carrying the "Essayons" device, that was excavated in the area behind the "Long Barracks," which burned in 1825. Another such button excavated at Sackets Harbor on the site of an 1812–1815 barracks bears a maker's name (Wishart) of the 1812–1816 period.

WAIST-BELT PLATE, GENERAL AND STAFF OFFICERS, 1832(?)–1850

USNM 604145-M (S–K 301). Figure 74.

This buckle is similar to the one (shown in fig. 73) that belonged to Capt. Charles O. Collins, but it is different in that the letters "u.s." are enclosed not by a laurel wreath but by a sprig of laurel on the right side and a sprig of palm on the left. The 1841 uniform regulations specified such a belt plate for officers of the Corps of Engineers, but with a "turreted castle, raised in silver" rather than the letters "u.s." This

FIGURE 74.—Specimen in Valley Forge Chapel Museum, Valley Forge, Pennsylvania.

places the probable date of manufacture of this specimen in the 1840's.

COAT-SKIRT ORNAMENT, GENERAL STAFF, 1832

USNM 8040. Figure 75.

This skirt ornament, on buff cloth, is from a coat worn by Capt. Thomas Swords when he was assistant quartermaster general in 1838. The design consists of three 6-pointed stars of gold bullion cord: a line

FIGURE 75

star of twisted cord superimposed upon a larger star of closely stitched cord that in turn is superimposed upon a still larger star of sunburst type.

COAT-SKIRT ORNAMENT, GENERAL STAFF, 1832

USNM 62057–M (S–K 181). Figure 76.

Like the preceding specimen, this ornament, on buff cloth, is comprised of three stars. A star made of lines of sequins secured by two strands of twisted

FIGURE 76

bullion is superimposed upon a 6-pointed star of gold embroidery that in turn is superimposed upon a 6-pointed star made up of gold sequins secured by gold bullion cord.

COAT-SKIRT ORNAMENT, ARTILLERY OFFICER, 1832

USNM 15929. Figure 77.

This specimen, on red cloth, is on a coat worn by William Tecumseh Sherman when he was a lieutenant in the 3d Artillery. The bomb is made of whorls of gold bullion cord, while the flames are composed of

curving lines of twisted bullion. The lowest flame on either side terminates in arrow heads.

There are a number of gold-embroidered shell and flame devices in the national collections, all varying considerably in size and composition. Some

FIGURE 77

are skirt ornaments for artillery officers, both Regular Army and Militia, while some are cap ornaments for ordnance officers. Indeed, two coats formerly belonging to Maj. Levi Twiggs, U.S. Marine Corps, carry the same device.

COAT-SKIRT ORNAMENT, INFANTRY OFFICER, 1832

USNM 59861–M. Figure 78.

The silver coat-skirt horn ornaments of infantry officers varied almost as much as the shell and flame devices, generally in relation to the affluence of the individual concerned. Unlike such ornaments of the other services, the horns were paired in rights and lefts on the coat.

This specimen, of silver bullion cord, is on a coat that once belonged to Lt. William Williams Mather, an 1828 graduate of the Military Academy who left the service in 1836. The horn is looped, and it is suspended by twisted bullion from a simple 3-leaf-clover knot. The whole is backed on blue cloth.

41

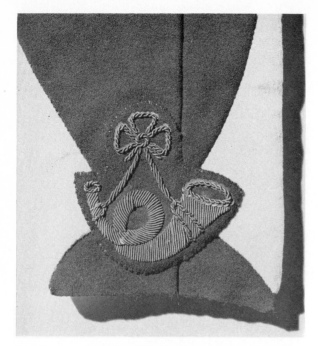

FIGURE 78

COAT-SKIRT ORNAMENT, INFANTRY OFFICER, 1832

USNM 1056. Figure 79.

This rather elaborate specimen is on a coat worn by John Porter Hatch when he was a lieutenant of infantry in 1845. The body of the horn—which is merely curved rather than looped—is made of silver lamé encircled by three ornamented bands of bullion.

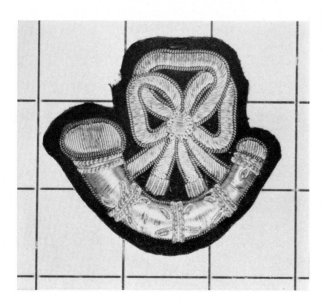

FIGURE 79

The mouthpiece and bell are of bullion. The whole is suspended by a rather ornate 3-leaf-clover knot of bands of edged bullion and is backed on blue cloth.

COAT-SKIRT ORNAMENT, CORPS OF TOPOGRAPHICAL ENGINEERS, 1839(?)

USNM 22702. Figure 80.

The uniform regulations for the period 1832–1846 carry no mention of coat-skirt ornaments for the Corps of Topographical Engineers, rather only prescribing the "slashed skirt flaps to be embroidered in gold, with oak leaves and acorns" like the collar and cuffs. There is in the national collections, however, a uniform for the Corps that corresponds with 1839 regulations in every way except that the coat skirts carry this ornament—a shield within a wreath of oak leaves—of gold embroidery. The device appears to be of the same vintage as the other embroidery on the coat.

FIGURE 80

¶ Although the 1832 uniform regulations make no mention of swords for noncommissioned officers, in 1833 the Ames Manufacturing Company of Chicopee, Massachusetts, began the manufacture of a new sword for the Regular artillery. Based on a European pattern, this weapon was the popular conception of the short Roman stabbing sword, or *gladius*. In 1834 this weapon was also authorized for infantry non-commissioned officers.[92]

[92] *Regulations for the Government of the Ordnance Department*, p. 64; and HAROLD L. PETERSON, pp. 42–43

WAIST-BELT PLATE, ARTILLERY NONCOMMISSIONED OFFICER, 1833

USNM 604384 (S–K 531). Figure 81.

This is the belt-plate assembly designed for carrying the short "Roman pattern" NCO sword. The plate is of two round pieces joined by an S-hook that is open on one end for unbuckling. Each round piece has a flat loop for attachment to the white buff belt. The right-hand round piece has an eagle with head to the left, wings drooping, three arrows in the right

FIGURE 82

FIGURE 81

talon, and an olive branch in the left talon. The left-hand piece has crossed cannons and the letters "U.S." The whole is cast in rough bronze.

Assemblies of this type were popularly known as "Dingee" belts, because one of the primary contractors for them was Robert Dingee of New York City. The eagle on this plate is very similar to the one on Dingee's contract rifle flasks of 1832.[93]

WAIST-BELT PLATE, INFANTRY NONCOMMISSIONED OFFICER, 1834

USNM 604111 (S–K 267). Figure 82.

This plate and belt are identical to the artillery specimen above except that the left-hand round portion exhibits three stacked muskets and a drum instead of crossed cannon.

¶ NCO belt plates similar to the two above also appeared in what might be called a staff or branch immaterial pattern, with the crossed cannon and/or

---

[93] See PATTERSON, p. 8.

FIGURE 83.—Specimen in collection of William E. Codd, Towson, Maryland.

stacked muskets and drum replaced by the letters "US" alone (fig. 83). This pattern apparently was intended for wear by NCO's other than those assigned to the infantry, artillery, or dragoons.

WAIST-BELT PLATE, DRAGOON OFFICER, 1833

USNM 5664. Figure 84.

This plate, which formerly belonged to Gen. William S. Harney when he commanded the 2d Dragoons in 1836, is identical to the general and staff officers' plate of the 1832 regulations except that the letters "U.S." have been replaced by the letter "D" in Old English, as prescribed.[94]

---

[94] General Order No. 38, Headquarters of the Army, May 2, 1833 (photostatic copy in files of the division of military history, Smithsonian Institution).

FIGURE 84

WAIST-BELT PLATE, NONCOMMISSIONED OFFICER, 1836

USNM 604114-M (S–K 268). Figure 85.

The 1835 uniform regulations replaced the rather impractical S-hook NCO belt plate with a "round clasp" on which the branch designation was replaced with the raised letters "u s." Similar in over-all design to the 1821 officers' plate, round with outer ring, these plates were rough cast in brass and had a stippled surface.

FIGURE 85

WAIST-BELT PLATE, NONCOMMISSIONED OFFICER, 1836

USNM 604114 (S–K 270). Not illustrated.

This specimen is very similar to the preceding plate, but it is of a definitely different casting and is generally heavier in over-all appearance, the inner ring is much more convex, and the letters "u s" are raised only slightly and spread farther apart.

SHOULDER-BELT PLATE, OFFICERS, 1839

USNM 40886. Figure 86.

The 1839 uniform regulations specified a shoulder belt (rather than a waist belt) for carrying the sword, with a "breast plate according to the pattern to be furnished by the Ordnance Department." This plate, which was worn by Capt. Erastus Capron, 1st Artillery, an 1833 graduate of the Military Academy, is believed to be that specified.[95] The specimen is rectangular with beveled edges, cast in brass, and has

FIGURE 86

[95] *U.S. Military Magazine* (April 1841), illustrations for "United States Infantry, Full Dress" and "United States Artillery (Captain)."

the lines of a modified sunburst radiating outward. In the center, within a wreath of laurel, are the letters "u s" in Old English. Both the wreath and letters are of silvered copper and are applied. The plate is attached by three broad hooks rather than two studs and a hook.

SHOULDER-BELT PLATE, OFFICERS, 1839

USNM 604330 (S–K 486). Not illustrated.

This plate is almost identical to the Capron specimen above except that the letters "u s," instead of being in Old English, are formed of oak leaves.

WAIST-BELT PLATE, CORPS OF TOPOGRAPHICAL ENGINEERS, 1839

USNM 22702. Figure 87.

The 1839 uniform regulations prescribed this plate for the Corps of Topographical Engineers. The oval inner plate, which contains the prescribed eagle,

FIGURE 87

shield, and the letters "u s" in Old English, is struck in medium weight copper and gilded. This inner plate is soldered to a cast-bronze and gilded tongue which in turn is brazed to a cast-bronze belt attachment. The oval outer ring, bearing the prescribed "CORPS OF TOPOGRAPHICAL ENGINEERS" in Roman capitals, is cast in brass and gilded. To the inner edge of this outer ring are brazed two curved seats for the inner oval. The whole is brazed to the belt attachment, also cast in brass and gilded.

¶ In view of the large and somewhat elaborate cap plates as well as shoulder-belt plates adopted by both the Regulars and Militia early in the 19th century, it is somewhat surprising that apparently neither component had ornamentation on its cartridge boxes until the Ordnance Regulations of 1834 prescribed a very ornate design embossed on the leather flap.[96] Certainly there was precedent for such, for both the British and German mercenary troops of the Revolution and the British and Canadian troops of the War of 1812 wore metal ornaments on their cartridge boxes. At least partial explanation for this omission may lie in one of Callender Irvine's reasons for rejecting brass cartridge boxes in favor of leather ones: "The leather . . . affords no mark for the enemy to sight at. The brass . . . would afford a central object, as regards the body of the Soldier, and one which would be seen at a great distance to fire at."[97] Why Irvine did not object equally to the large white and yellow metal cap and shoulder-belt plates as targets is unknown. In any case—with a possible few Militia exceptions such as a Militia cartridge box with a plate bearing the likeness of Washington in silver, both about 1835—the 1839 model oval plates were the first to be worn.

The ordnance regulations of 1839 and the ordnance manual of 1841 brought in two distinctly new types of plates, the familiar brass oval waist-belt and cartridge-box plates with the letters "u. s." and the round shoulder-belt plate with the eagle. The oval plates fall into two general sizes, 3.5 inches by 2.2 inches (for plates on the infantry's cartridge box and the cavalry's waist belts)[98] and 2.8 inches by 1.6 inches (for plates on the infantry's waist belts and the cavalry's carbine cartridge boxes and pistol cartridge boxes). The use of each plate is determined by the type of fastener. These plates were struck in thin brass and the backs generally leaded, although some were used without such backing, probably to save both weight and material. Cartridge boxes were also embossed with the outline of this oval plate in lieu of the plate itself. It is interesting to note that the larger plates with lead backs weighed about 5½ ounces and the smaller ones just over 2 ounces.

---

[96] See *Military Collector and Historian* (June 1950), vol. 2, no. 2, pp. 29–30.

[97] Letter dated June 29, 1813, from Irvine to Secretary of War (Records AGO).

[98] The cavalry waist-belt plate is actually specified to be 3.6 inches by 2.2 inches.

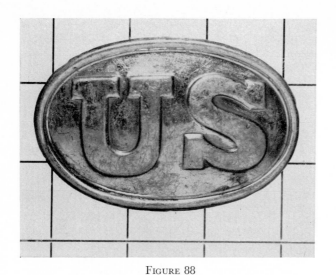

FIGURE 88

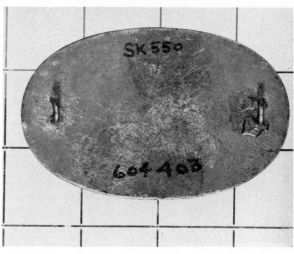

FIGURE 90

WAIST-BELT PLATE, CAVALRY, 1839

USNM 604408 (S–K 555). Figures 88, 89.

The specimen is oval, slightly convex, and struck in thin brass. The face has a raised edge and the letters "u s." The reverse is leaded, carries two studs and a hook (indicating its use), and is stamped with the maker's name, "W. H. Smith, Brooklyn." Smith is listed in New York City directories of the Civil War period as a contractor for metal and leather supplies.

contractor in the New York City area in the Civil War period.

CARTRIDGE-BOX PLATE, CAVALRY, 1839

USNM 604395 (S–K 542). Not illustrated.

This is the oval "u s" plate of the smaller size (2¾ by 1⅛ in.), otherwise identical to the larger plate. It is fitted with two looped-wire fasteners.

WAIST-BELT PLATE, INFANTRY, 1839

USNM 604398 (S–K 545). Figure 91.

This specimen is identical to the preceding plate except that it is fitted with two brass hooks for attachment to the belt and the reverse is stamped with the maker's name, "Boyd & Sons." No trace of a manufacturer of such products by the name of Boyd

FIGURE 89

CARTRIDGE-BOX PLATE, INFANTRY, 1839

USNM 604403 (S–K 550). Figure 90.

This plate is identical to the preceding one except that it is leaded and fitted with two looped-wire fasteners. The reverse is stamped with the name of the maker, "J. L. Pittman," who, like Smith, was a

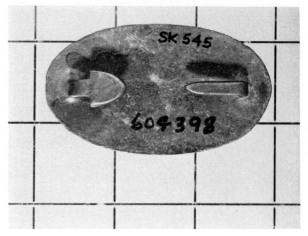

FIGURE 91

has been found. It is probable that he worked during the Civil War period when there were many such contractors.

WAIST-BELT PLATE, INFANTRY, 1839

USNM 604399 (S–K 546). Not illustrated.

This plate is identical to those above except that the reverse is stamped with the maker's name, "H. A. Dingee."

WAIST-BELT PLATE, INFANTRY, 1839

USNM 604397 (S–K 544). Figure 92.

The reverse side of this plate is fitted with the rather rudimentary wire fasteners similar to those on shoulder-belt plates of the 1812–1821 period. In other respects the specimen is identical to the preceding ones of 1839.

¶ The 1839 regulations specified a bayonet-belt plate "round, brass, with eagle." The 1841 ordnance manual was more exact, specifying the plate to be "brass, circular, 2.5 in. diameter, with an Eagle," and then stating: "The bayonet belt is about to be discontinued . . . ." Although not so authorized at the time, this plate, so familiar during the Civil War period, was switched over to the shoulder belt supporting the cartridge box. Such plates were manufactured in great quantities and in many variations of the original design by a dozen or more contractors during the period 1861–1865.

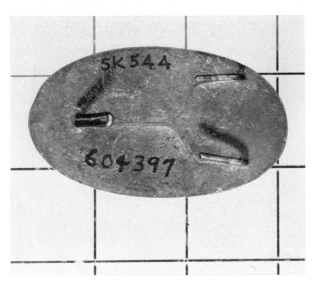

FIGURE 92

CARTRIDGE-BOX-BELT PLATE, 1839

USNM 60338–M (S–K 94). Figure 93.

This circular plate, with raised rim, is dominated by an eagle of refined design that is very similar to the eagles appearing on the War of 1812 plates. The eagle has its wings drooped, head to the left, three arrows in the right talon, and an olive branch in the left talon. This specimen can be dated with the earliest cartridge-box plates because of its backing and the type of fasteners. Whereas the backs of the later models were lead-filled, this plate was struck in thin brass over tin and the edges of the obverse crimped to retain the backing. The fasteners are of the bent-wire type typical of the 1812–1832 period and are not the "2 eyes of iron wire" called for in the ordnance manual of 1850. None of the later examples of this design evidence any of the refinement of the original. At least eight variations are represented in the national collections.

CARTRIDGE-BOX-BELT PLATE, 1839, DIE SAMPLE

USNM 60339–M (S–K 95). Not illustrated.

This is a die sample, struck in copper, of the plate described above.

SWORD-BELT PLATE, 1851

USNM 38017. Figures 94, 95.

The 1851 regulations prescribed this plate for all officers and enlisted men. It was specified to be "gilt, rectangular, two inches wide, with a raised bright rim; a silver wreath of laurel encircling the 'Arms of the United States'; eagle, scroll, edge of cloud and rays bright. The motto, 'E Pluribus Unum,' in silver letters upon the scroll; stars also of silver; according to pattern." [99]

This plate has had a longer history than any other similar Army device. It was authorized for all personnel until 1881 when it was dropped as an item of enlisted equipment. It was retained for officers, first for general wear, then for dress only. It was worn with officers' dress blue uniforms until 1941, but was not revived when blues reappeared after World War II. A plate of the same general size and pattern, although gilt in its entirety, was prescribed for senior NCO's of the Marine Corps until about 1950 or 1951.

The buckle appears in many variations of design, at least 12 being represented in the national collec-

---

[99] *Regulations for the Uniform and Dress,* pl. 21.

FIGURE 93

FIGURE 94

FIGURE 95

tions. Many of these variations are the result of the plate being produced in great numbers by many different contractors during the Civil War. The original design itself is interesting. The 1851 description called for an "edge of cloud and rays" and the official, full size drawing in *Regulations for the Uniform and Dress of the Army* includes the "edge of cloud" and pictures the eagle with its head to the heraldic left. At least 50 of these plates were examined by the authors, but only this specimen had the "edge of cloud," silver letters and stars, and the eagle with its head to the left. In most specimens the plate proper is bronze, in one piece, and with the wreath silvered or left plain; in a few specimens the wreath is in white metal and has been applied after casting. This particular specimen is of an early issue. It is cast in heavy brass, with the wreath applied, and has the narrow brass tongue for attachment on the reverse (fig. 95), typical of the early types.

SWORD-BELT PLATE, 1851, DIE SAMPLE

USNM 60342–M (S-K 98). Figure 96.

This is a sample struck from a die which apparently was not approved for the 1851 pattern plate. The eagle has wings upraised (2 inches tip to tip), head

FIGURE 96

to right, shield on breast, scroll with "E Pluribus Unum" in beak, three arrows in right talon, and an olive branch in left talon. Stars are intermixed with "edge of cloud" and rays.

The specimen leads to the interesting speculation as to the weight given to correct heraldic usage at this period. The significance of the clouds, or lack of them, is unknown, but it should be noted that in all but the earliest specimens the eagle's head is turned to the right, or the side of honor, and the olive branch is placed in the right talon, indicating peaceful national motives as opposed to the three arrows, signs of belligerency, in the left talon. In this respect, it is interesting to note that until 1945 the eagle on the President's seal and flag carried its head turned to the heraldic left.

Insignia of the Uniformed Militia

Cap and Helmet Devices

HAT ORNAMENT, INDEPENDENT DRAGOONS(?), C. 1800

USNM 14978. Figure 97.

This silver ornament is one of the most unusual pieces of military insignia in the national collections. Obviously military, it is just as obviously of Militia origin. Although hardly artistic in design, it has a rather attractive simplicity and has been made with considerable care. The eagle is of the "frogleg" design that first appeared on buttons of the post-Revolutionary Army and, later on, of the Legion. In its right talon the eagle is grasping what appear to be rather stylized thunderbolts, and in its left, arrows. The arc above the eagle's head is comprised of sunrays, an edge of clouds, and 16 6-pointed stars. If the number of stars is of significance, the piece would date prior to November 1802 when the 17th state, Ohio, was admitted to the union. The "frog-legged" aspect of the design would tend to confirm such dating, and the thunderbolts in the right talon, symbolic of a belligerent attitude, could be attributed to the national temper during the "quasi war" with France, 1798–1800. The "ID," in delicate floriated script on the eagle's breast, quite out of consonance with the design and execution of the piece proper and obviously the work of a talented engraver, is interpreted as "Independent Dragoons." Too small for a hat frontpiece, it was probably worn as a side ornament on a dragoon helmet.

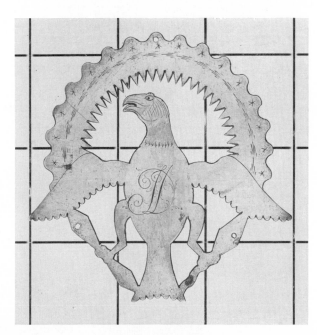

FIGURE 97

LEATHER FAN COCKADE, C. 1810

USNM 60257–M (S–K 15). Figure 98.

The leather fan cockade became a part of the uniform in the late 18th century, having evolved from the cloth cockade adopted early in the Revolution.[100] Enlisted men's cockades of the early 19th century were of leather, as were those of line officers.[101] This cockade, of black tooled leather

[100] FINKE, pp. 71–73.
[101] TODD, "Three Leather Cockades," pp. 24–25.

FIGURE 98

with painted gold fan tips, was a common form of the period and was worn with an eagle in the center or possibly on the upper fan. It is assigned to the Militia because of the gold ornamentation.

CAP PLATE, C. 1810

USNM 60275–M (S–K 33). Figure 99.

This grenadier-type plate, which is untrimmed and thus may be a die sample, is a rare example of the use of coiled snakes as a military device after 1800. A familiar motif of the Revolution, coiled snakes were not revived as a popular military symbol during the War of 1812. This specimen is struck in brass and is believed to have been made for a specific independent Militia organization, designation unknown, for wear prior to 1812.

COCKADE EAGLE, 1812–1815

USNM 60361–M (S–K 117). Figure 100.

The eagle-on-clouds design, which first appeared on coins on the 1795 silver dollar, was popular on insignia during the period 1812–1821. The heraldic significance of the clouds, if any, is unknown. Somewhat larger than most cockade devices, this eagle is

FIGURE 99

FIGURE 100

FIGURE 101

struck in brass and silvered and has two simple wire fasteners soldered to the reverse. A very similar badge is shown by Rembrant Peale in an oil portrait of Col. Joseph O. Bogart of the 3d Flying Artillery.[102]

COCKADE EAGLE, C. 1814

USNM 60379-M (S-K 135). Figure 101.

This eagle, of the general design first seen on the 1807 half-dollar, is very similar to the one on buttons ascribed to staff officers, 1814–1821.[103] The eagle, struck in brass, has wings upraised and the familiar hooked beak; it stands on a wreath of the colors. The wire fasteners on the reverse are of a somewhat unusual type and may not be contemporary.

¶ Die work for cap, shoulder-belt, and waist-belt plates was expensive, and many Militia organizations found it expedient to purchase devices "ready made" from existing dies. By varying the trimming and adding borders of various designs, the same dies could

---

[102] Reproduced in *Antiques* (July 1947), vol. 52, no. 7, p. 16.
[103] JOHNSON, specimen nos. 101–105.

be used to strike all three types of plates. Such badges are called "common" plates.

The common plates that follow were very popular during the period 1812–1835 and, although relatively rare today, were made in considerable quantity and in many die variations for the Militia in every part of the country. They are known in brass, copper, and silver-on-copper. It is possible that specimens such as these may have been worn by some officers of the Regular Establishment between 1814 and 1821.

CAP PLATE, 1814–1825(?)

USNM 60263-M (S-K 21). Figure 102.

This is a typical example of the common plates of the 1814–1835 period. The piece is struck in brass and has an edged and stippled border. The design is dominated by an eagle with wings outspread, head to left, arrows in right talon, olive branch in left talon, and with the national motto on a ribbon overhead. The whole is superimposed on a trophy of arms and colors with an arc of 13 6-pointed stars above. A plume socket, apparently original, is soldered to the reverse, as are two looped-wire fasteners. The fasteners are of a later period.

FIGURE 102

FIGURE 103

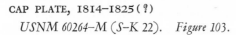

CAP PLATE, 1814–1825 (?)

USNM 60264–M (S–K 22). Figure 103.

Struck in copper and silvered, this piece is a die variant of the preceding plate. A floral border replaces the plain border, and the overhead arc has 5-pointed rather than 6-pointed stars. The floral border marks it as probably an officer's device.

CAP PLATE, 1814–1825 (?)

USNM 60313–M (S–K 69). Figure 104.

A die variant of the preceding plate, this device has an unusually wide floral border. As in so many of the common pieces of this period, the center device was purposely designed small so that the die could be used to strike matching waist-belt plates. Examples of waist-belt plates struck from dies of this particular design are known. Struck in copper, there is a plume socket soldered to the reverse along with two looped-wire fasteners. The fasteners are not contemporary.

CAP PLATE, 1814–1825 (?)

USNM 60314–M (S–K 70). Figure 105.

This is a die variant of the three plates immediately preceding. However, the center device lacks the fineness of detail of the others, a fact that suggests that several makers working with different die sinkers produced this basic pattern. The plate is struck in copper, and originally it had a plume socket attached to the reverse. The present looped-wire fasteners are not original.

CAP PLATE, 1814–1825 (?)

USNM 60299–M (S–K 57). Figure 106.

This plate, which is of brass, is of a less common design than its predecessors. However, since there is another such plate, but of silver-on-copper, in the national collections, it can be surmised that pieces of this same pattern were made for use by several different units.

A floral-bordered shield is topped by an out-sized sunburst with 13 stars, clouds, and the motto "Unity

↑ FIGURE 104

FIGURE 105 ↓

FIGURE 106

is Strength." In the center of the shield is the eagle, with wings widely outspread and with lightning bolts in the right talon and an olive branch in the left talon. The lightning bolt device, obvious sign of belligerency, first appeared about 1800 and is not seen in plates designed after 1821. The motto and the date 1776 are far more typical of Militia than Regular Army usage.

¶ In 1821 the Regular Army discarded all its large cap plates and adopted the bell-crown leather cap. Militia organizations lost no time in adopting a similar cap and, conversely, placing on it—and on the tall beaver which followed in the 1830's—the largest plates it could accommodate, using variations of discarded Regular Army patterns as well as original designs.

From 1821 until well into the 1840's large cap plates were mass-produced by manufacturers in Boston, New York, Philadelphia, and perhaps other cities of the New England metal manufacturing area. The few early platemakers, such as Crumpton and Armitage of Philadelphia and Peasley of Boston, were

55

joined by a number of others. Prominent among these were Charles John Joullain, who made plates in New York during the 1820's, and William Pinchin of Philadelphia. Joullain is first listed in New York directories, in 1817, as a "gilder," and so continues through 1828. Sometimes his given name is listed as Charles, sometimes as James, and finally as Charles James. From 1820 to 1828 his address is the same, 32 Spring Street. There is a William Pinchin (Pinchon) listed in the Philadelphia directories as a silverplater or silversmith almost continuously from 1785 through 1863, indicating the possibility of a family occupation.

It is believed that some of the New England makers of uniform buttons also manufactured plates. Among such buttonmakers of the 1820's and 1830's were R. and W. Robinson, D. Evans and Co., Leavenworth and Co., Benedict and Coe, and others in Connecticut and Massachusetts. Buttonmakers often stamped their names or easily recognizable hallmarks on the back of their products.

In most cases it is virtually impossible to ascertain the precise units for which these different plates were first designed, and the problem is further complicated because the maker would sell a specific plate design to several different units. Those designs that incorporate all or part of a state's seal were originally made for Militia organizations of the particular state, but in several instances these plates were sold—altered or not—to units in other parts of the country. Militia organizations that were widely separated geographically purchased cap plates from distant manufacturers who had perhaps a dozen or more stock patterns to offer at a cost much lower than that involved in making a new die from which to strike custom-made ornaments. It made no difference to the Savannah Greys, in Georgia, that their new cap plates were the same as those worn by organizations in Pennsylvania and Massachusetts. Toward the end of this period of large cap plates, manufacturers came out with two-piece ornaments. After 1833, when the Regiment of United States Dragoons was authorized its large sunburst plate with separate eagle ornament in the center, insignia makers introduced a veritable rash of full sunburst, three-quarter sunburst, and half-sunburst cap plates with interchangeable centers. And for the first time small Militia units could afford their own distinctive devices at little extra cost. Shoulder-belt and waist-belt plates underwent the same evolution, and by the late 1830's such plates had become a mix-

ture of either single die stampings or composite plates made of several parts soldered or otherwise held onto a rectangular or oval background.

Study of cap plates and other insignia in the Huddy and Duval prints in *U.S. Military Magazine* points to the years between 1833 and perhaps 1837 or 1838 as the transition period from single to composite ornaments, years during which there was also tremendous growth in the popularity and number of independent Militia units. In contrast to the 1820's when the Militia often waited until the Regulars discarded a device before adopting it, in 1840 there were no less than five organizations, mounted and dismounted, wearing the 1833 dragoon plate in full form while it was still in use by the Regulars. *U.S. Military Magazine* illustrates such plates for the Richmond Light Infantry Blues, the Georgia Hussars, the Macon Volunteers, the Jackson Rifle Corps of Lancaster, Pa., the Montgomery Light Guard, and the Harrison Guards of Allentown, Pa. The plate of the Harrison Guards is an example of the license sometimes practiced by Huddy and Duval in the preparation of their military prints. The color bearer in this print is depicted wearing a full sunburst plate, while the description of the uniform called for "a semicircular plate or *gloria*." [104]

In the following descriptions of plates, the term "stock pattern" is used because the insignia are known to have been worn by more than one organization, because their basic designs are so elementary that it appears obvious that they were made for wide distribution, or because they are known to have been made both in silver and in gilt metals.

CAP PLATE, ARTILLERY, C. 1825
USNM 60307-M (S-K 64). Figure 107.

On the raised center of this shield-shaped plate is the eagle-on-cannon device within an oval floral border; the Federal shield is below. The whole is superimposed on a trophy of arms and colors with portions of a modified sunburst appearing on the sides. The plate is struck in brass. The eagle-on-cannon first appeared on Regular artillery buttons in 1802. About 1808 it was used as an embossed device on the leather fan cockade, and in 1814 it became the principal design element of the cap plate for

---

[104] *U.S. Military Magazine* (March 1839), p. 4.

FIGURE 107

Regulars. This plate is thought to be one of the earliest of the post–1821 series of Militia cap plates incorporating the discarded design of the Regular artillery.

UNIDENTIFIED ORNAMENT, PROBABLY CAP PLATE, C. 1821

USNM 60331–M (S–K 87). Figure 108.

This silver-on-copper plate is unique in size, shape, and over-all design. It is one of the most unusual Militia insignia in the national collections. The standing eagle of the 1807 mint design with Federal shield, the panoply of arms and colors, and the rayed background all suggest that this plate was made not later than the early 1820's. Quite possibly it is a cap plate of the War of 1812 period, but positive dating is impossible. Three simple wire fasteners are affixed to the reverse.

CAP PLATE, ARTILLERY, C. 1825

USNM 60255–M (S–K 13). Figure 109.

Although the Regular riflemen wore a diamond-shaped plate from 1812 to 1814, this shape does not appear on Militia caps until the mid-1820's. It was a common form through the 1830's, but since it was always made as a one-piece die-struck plate it became out-dated in the late 1830's when the composite plates came into vogue.

This plate, struck in brass and bearing the eagle-on-cannon device, must be considered a stock pattern available to many organizations. Insignia struck from the same die could have been easily made into shoulder-belt plates as well.

FIGURE 108

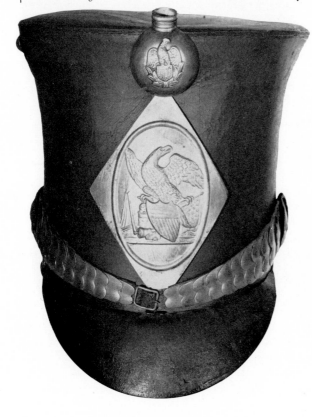

↑ FIGURE 109   FIGURE 110 ↓

CAP PLATE AND PLUME HOLDER, C. 1825

USNM 604748 (S–K 893). Figure 110.

This brass plate is similar in many respects to the regular infantry cap plate, type I, 1814–1821. It is attached to a bell-crowned shako of distinctly Militia origin and is cut in the diamond shape popular with the Militia in the 1820's and 1830's. The design lies within a raised oval dominated by an eagle similar to ones used on War of 1812 insignia. Below the eagle is a Federal shield and a trophy of stacked muskets, a drum surmounted by a dragoon helmet, a gun on a truck carriage, and colors—one the National Colors with 16 stars in the canton.

The plume holder attached to the cap above the plate is an unusually interesting and distinctive device. It is a hemisphere of thin brass with a round plume socket at the top. The hemisphere has an eagle on a shield and a superimposed wreath device in silver. The blazonry of the shield cannot be identified with any particular state or locality.

CAP PLATE, C. 1821

USNM 60262 (S–K 20). Figure 111.

The familiar hooked-beak eagle dominates the center of this brass, scalloped-edge plate. The arrows of belligerency, however, are held in the left talon. Surrounding the eagle is a three-quarter wreath of olive with the national motto above and the date 1776 below. While there is a possibility that this plate may fall into the period 1814–1821 because of its outline shape, it lacks the panoply of arms associated with that era. It is much more probable that this is one of the earliest plates made for Militia during the years 1821–1830. Since this plate is also known in silver-on-copper, it is considered a stock pattern.

CAP PLATE, MILITIA, ARTILLERY (?), C. 1821

USNM 60306–M (S–K 63). Figure 112.

This oval, brass-struck plate framed within a large wreath of laurel is one of the finest in the national collections, comprising as it does a number of devices of excellent design and considerable detail standing in high relief. The curving line of 21 stars above the motto, decreasing in size laterally, is an interesting detail, and the eagle and panoply of arms is reminiscent of those on the plate ascribed to the Regiment of Light Artillery, 1814–1821, and on several of the common Militia plates of the same period. It is

58

FIGURE 111   FIGURE 112

assigned to the artillery because of its "yellow metal" composition. It has simple wire fasteners, applied to the reverse, and carries no plume socket.

CAP PLATE, NEW YORK, C. 1825

USNM 60273–M (S–K 31). *Figure 113.*

This unusually large, shield-shaped plate, struck in brass, is dominated by an eagle—within a smaller shield with raised edge—standing on a half globe and wreath of the colors, both of which are super-imposed on a trophy of arms and flags; clouds and sun rays are above. The specimen represents one of the large cap plate patterns adopted by the Militia for wear on the bell-crown cap soon after it came into general use in the early 1820's. While a stock pattern in a sense, its use was most likely confined to New York State Militia because its principal device, the eagle-on-half-globe, is taken directly from that state's seal. These large plates were widely worn until the middle or late 1830's when newer styles began to replace them. The plume socket affixed to the reverse appears to be contemporary, but has been resoldered.

CAP PLATE, NEW YORK, C. 1825

USNM 60356–M (S–K 112). *Figure 114.*

This is a variant of the preceding plate and well illustrates how an insignia-maker could adapt a single die for several products. The eagle-on-half-globe, with a portion of the trophy of arms and colors, and the clouds and sunburst above have merely been cut out from the plate proper for use alone. The plate is struck in brass.

Another specimen, of silver-on-copper, is known, indicating that this insignia was made for wear by infantry as well as by other branches of the service; consequently, it may be termed a stock pattern.

CAP PLATE, NEW YORK, C. 1825

USNM 60266–M (S–K 24). *Figure 115.*

Illustrating fine craftsmanship, this elaborate brass cap plate comprises perhaps the most ornate and intricately detailed design ever attempted by a military ornament die sinker. The strike itself has been so well executed that the most minute details are

59

FIGURE 113

FIGURE 114

even today readily discernible, even after very apparent use. Made for New York Militia, its central theme is the eagle-on-half-globe superimposed on a trophy of arms and flags.

Many of the facets of detail are of particular interest. Almost every ray of the aura of sunlight can still be clearly seen; the North Pole is well marked with a vertical arrow; the Arctic Circle, Tropic of Capricorn, and the Equator are included on the half-globe, as are the meridians of longitude and the parallels of latitude; both North America and South America are shown, and that portion of North America east of the Mississippi basin is clearly denominated "UNITED STATES." An unusual feature of the design is the way the arrows are held in the eagle's left talon—some of the arrow heads point inward, some outward. What appears to have been a contemporary plume socket has been resoldered to the reverse.

Although this plate is unmarked as to maker, another plate of a similar design but of silver-on-copper has the maker's mark "J. JOULLAIN, MAKER, N.

YORK." Since two distinct but similar designs are known, and the finished product is found in both brass and silver-on-copper, it seems probable that this plate was produced by more than one maker, and for all arms of the service. It is therefore deemed a stock pattern.

CAP PLATE, RIFLEMEN, C. 1825

USNM 60267–M (S–K 25). Figure 116.

Almost immediately after the last Regular rifle regiment was disbanded in 1821, Militia riflemen adopted the large open horn with loops and tassels that the Regulars had worn from 1817 to 1821. The basic device was altered slightly by showing an eagle in flight and the horn suspended much lower on its cords. The illustrated brass plate is one of four die variants, and more than a dozen similar to it have been examined. It is significant that all are of brass, for these were made and worn during the period when the trimmings for infantry were silver or "white metal."

This plate differs from the others examined in that it has 17 6-pointed stars along the upper and lower parts of the shield inside the border. The number of stars cannot be significant in dating for the plate was

↑ FIGURE 115

obviously made long after 1812 when the 18th state, Louisiana, was admitted to the Union. A plume socket affixed to the reverse appears to be original.

Undoubtedly made as a stock pattern by several manufacturers, these plates continued in use for at least 15 years after they first appeared about 1825. Although *U.S. Military Magazine* illustrates many large cap plates for the period 1839–1841, none has a shield outline. This may indicate a decline in the popularity of the design, but it must be remembered that Huddy and Duval presented the uniforms of only a small cross-section of the Militia of the period.

CAP PLATE, RIFLEMEN, C. 1825

USNM 60267–M (S–K 26). Figure 117.

This is a second form of Militia riflemen's plates. Struck in brass, it differs from the preceding primarily in the placement of 17 5-pointed stars along the upper half of the shield, between the borders. Other small differences show that the basic die was not that used for the preceding specimen. The most obvious dif-

FIGURE 116 ↓

FIGURE 117

61

ference is the legend "E PLURIBUS UNUM" carried on
the ribbon behind the knotted cord of the horn, an
element not present in the other.

A third form, not illustrated, substitutes a floral
border for the plain border around the edge of the
shield and contains no stars as part of the design.
Still a fourth form, also not illustrated, has the same
center device of eagle and open horn placed in a
longer and narrower shield, with 23 6-pointed stars
between the borders.

¶ These various combinations of devices give a good
clue as to the method of manufacture of stock patterns,
and indicate the use of several different dies and hand
punches. The blank metal was first struck by a die
that formed the plain or floral border and cut the
outline of the plate. Next, a smaller die containing
the center device of eagle and horn was used. Then
the stars, and sometimes elements of the floral border,
were added by individual striking with a hand punch.
This latter method is clearly revealed by the comparison of several "identical" plates in which the
stars or elements of the border are irregularly and
differently spaced.

CAP PLATE, RIFLEMAN PATTERN, C. 1825

USNM 60398–M (S–K 154). Figure 118.

This plate is called "rifleman pattern" because it
is silver-on-copper and is the only known example
of this type of insignia made for wear by infantry,
or possibly for Militia riflemen whose trimmings were,
incorrectly, silver.

There are several conjectures about this cut-out
device made from a die of the preceding series of
shield plates. It may have been made after 1834,
when the open horn with cord and tassels was adopted
by the Regular infantry as a branch device. It is
equally possible that it was submitted to a Militia
infantry organization by some maker as a sample
during the 1820's and when selected was silvered to
conform with other trimmings. In either case, it
illustrates how a single die could serve to make many
different variations from a basic design.

CAP PLATE, RIFLEMEN, C. 1825

USNM 60304–M (S–K 61B). Figure 119.

The very unusual construction of this brass plate
for riflemen indicates that it is possibly one of the
earliest of the composite plates. Within a wreath

FIGURE 118

of crossed laurel boughs is a small center circle with
raised edge to which has been soldered the eagle
and horn device struck in convex form.

FIGURE 119

CAP PLATE, RIFLEMEN, C. 1830

USNM 60252–M (S–K 10). **Figure 120.**

The diamond-shaped plate was in vogue with Militia units during the late 1820's and the 1830's. Examples of such plates for the Washington Grays (Philadelphia) and the Philadelphia Grays are recorded in *U.S. Military Magazine.*[105] This brass plate, possibly made for a particular unit from stock dies, is a typical example of the endless variety possible with the use of a few dies. The blank was struck with a die for the center device of eagle and horn, but the irregularity of the spacing of the stars shows that they were added later by hand. Similar plates may be found with essentially this same device, but placed on small shields or backgrounds of other shapes.

CAP PLATE, C. 1835

USNM 604851–M (S–K 996). **Figure 121.**

The eagle and horn devices were sometimes separated by the manufacturer to produce this type ornament—open with cord and tassels. Struck in brass, it differs in form and detail from the silver horn adopted by the Regular infantry in 1834 as a cap plate.

Several Militia units of the late 1830's and 1840's used a horn as an additional ornament on the rear of the cap, notably the State Fencibles (Philadelphia) and the National Guard (Philadelphia). On the rear of the leather cap of the State Fencibles were "two broad rich stripes of silver lace, starting from the same point at the top and running down, forming an angle, in the center of which is a bugle ornament . . . ."[106] The cap of the National Guard has been described as being "of blue cloth . . . and in the rear a plated bugle ornament."[107]

¶ In the following series of rather similar plates, four different dies are used for the center ornament, perhaps made by as many different die sinkers. The relatively large number of these plates still in existence suggests that they were worn very extensively. Those with silver finish were used by infantry; the gilt or copper ones by artillery and perhaps by staff officers. All specimens are currently fitted with plain wire

---

[105] April 1839, pl. 5; June 1839, pl. 11.
[106] *U.S. Military Magazine* (March 1839), p. 3 and pl. 2.
[107] *U.S. Military Magazine* (October 1841), p. 32.

FIGURE 120

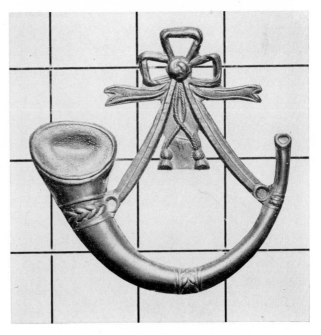

FIGURE 121

63

fasteners and plume sockets, both of which may or may not be original.

CAP PLATE, INFANTRY, C. 1825

USNM 60271–M (S–K 29). Figure 122.

The floral-bordered shield outline of this silver-on-copper infantry plate is known to have been used also with the rifleman's eagle-horn device in the center. The panoply of arms and flags used as a background for the center device, which is characterized by the long neck of the eagle swung far to the right, links it closely to the plate of similar type worn during the period 1814–1821. Because of its large size, it is assigned to the post-1821 era of the bell-crown cap, contemporary with the riflemen's large plates. The 13 5-pointed stars were added with a hand punch.

FIGURE 123

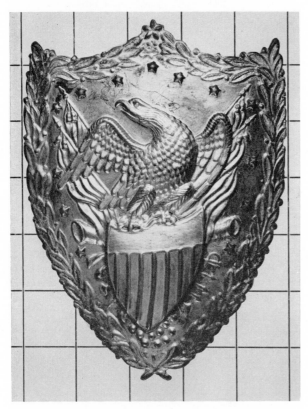

FIGURE 122

CAP PLATE, C. 1825

USNM 60298–M (S–K 56). Figure 123.

This brass plate is a duplicate of the preceding, lacking only the hand-applied stars. The crispness

of detail indicates that it was one of the very early products of the die.

CAP PLATE, C. 1825

USNM 60269–M (S–K 27). Figure 124.

The second variation of the series is a product of perhaps the best executed die of the group, with unusually fine detail in the eagle's wings and with neatly stacked cannon balls at the bottom of the center device. It includes other excellent detail not found in other dies: an eagle-head pommel on one sword, a star pattern made of smaller stars in the cantons of the flags, and crossed cannon, rammer, and worm behind the Federal shield. It is struck in brass.

CAP PLATE, C. 1825

USNM 60297–M (S–K 55). Figure 125.

A tall, slender, rather graceless eagle with broad wings and erect head reminiscent of the Napoleonic eagle is the outstanding difference in this third example of the series. The floral border lacks a finished

FIGURE 124

FIGURE 125

look because the plate, which is of brass, was apparently hand trimmed.

CAP PLATE, C. 1825

USNM 60270–M (S–K 28).   Figure 126.

This fourth variation, of silver-on-copper, bears an eagle with very small legs (somewhat out of proportion), an erect head, a fierce mien, and a heavy round breast. The design is struck on a shield-plate with the exact measurements as on one of the riflemen series.

CAP PLATE, MUSICIAN, C. 1825

USNM 60302–M (S–K 60).   Figure 127.

The oldest known plate made expressly for musicians, this silver-on-copper, floral-bordered shield bears an eagle similar to one for riflemen of the same period (see fig. 116). Among the early musical instruments easily identifiable in the design are the tambor, the serpent, the French horn, and the rack of bells. Such a plate was undoubtedly a stock pattern, available in either gilt or silver finish, and was probably sold well into the 1840's. The reverse is fitted with what

appears to be a contemporary plume socket, although resoldered, and two simple wire fasteners.

CAP PLATE, MUSICIAN, C. 1835

USNM 6030–M (S–K 61A).   Figure 128.

This gilded brass plate, while not as old as the preceding one, is of an unusual pattern. Made for New York State Militia, it carries the eagle-on-half-globe device at the top. The central design includes a French horn, a serpent, and a straight horn, all intertwined about an open roll of sheet music. It is probably a stock pattern. The reverse is fitted with three simple bent-wire fasteners.

CAP PLATE, C. 1830

USNM 60250–M (S–K 8).   Figure 129.

The design on this brass plate, reminiscent of that on the regular infantry cap plate, 1814–1821, was adopted for wear by the Militia after being discarded by the Regular Establishment. The ornate floral border and diamond shape place it in the late 1820's and the

↑ FIGURE 126   FIGURE 127 ↓

FIGURE 128

1830's, although the lightning in the eagle's left talon and the arrows in its right talon are usually associated with plates designed prior to 1821. It has been suggested that this is the plate worn by the West Point cadets after 1821, but such seems doubtful.

¶ No Militia plates enjoyed wider use or longer life than those patterned after the plate that disappeared from the Regular Establishment with the disbanding of the dragoons in 1815. More than a dozen die variants are known, several worn by more than one Militia unit. Although size and shape may vary, any plate exhibiting a mounted trooper with upraised saber can safely be assigned to mounted Militia However, the dating of such plates is a real problem because they are known to have been in use as late as 1861.

A Huddy and Duval print of the Washington Cavalry of Philadelphia County shows that unit

FIGURE 129

wearing a plate similar to the one used by the Regulars, differing only in its brass composition, as opposed to the original pewter of the 1812 regulations.[108] A cap in the collections of the Valley Forge Museum that was worn by a member of this unit in the period 1835–1845 is very similar to the one shown in the Huddy and Duval print. The cap is a copy of the 1812 Regular Army pattern, with somewhat more ornate brass bindings in place of the iron strips. A similar cap, carrying the label "Canfield and Bro., Baltimore," is owned by Lexington, Virginia, descendants of a member of the Rockbridge [Virginia] Dragoons. That unit is said to have worn such a cap upon first entering Confederate service in 1861.

In the national collections there is a dragoon cap (USNM 604767, S–K 912) carrying a plate of this design struck on a massive diamond-shaped piece with concave sides. There are additional variations in several private collections and at the Fort Ticonderoga Museum. The mounted horseman device was also struck on heart-shaped martingale ornaments.

---

[108] See *U.S. Military Magazine* (February 1840), pl. 29.

CAP PLATE, DRAGOONS, C. 1830

USNM 60254-M (S–K 12). Figure 130.

The horseman on this brass plate, designed with a rather crude, childlike simplicity, is garbed quite differently than the Regular dragoon on the 1812 pewter specimen. The plate is assigned to the general 1830 period to fit the era of the diamond-shaped plates, but its use doubtless continued on into the 1840's. By nature of its design it would have been a manufacturer's stock pattern.

CAP PLATE, ARTILLERY (?), C. 1830

USNM 60301–M (S–K 59). Figure 131.

The eagle on this brass plate is similar to the ones on the preceding shield plates, but the Federal shield on which he stands is ornamented with three star devices composed of smaller stars. An unusual feature of this plate is the addition of the flaming portion of a grenade rising from the eagle's head, a device not a part of any other known cap plate. This

FIGURE 130

FIGURE 131

FIGURE 132

symbol suggests artillery, and the plate is of the proper color. Although an unusual over-all design, the lack of any components of state arms or crests indicate that it may have been a stock pattern. The reverse is fitted with two simple bent-wire fasteners.

CAP PLATE, MASSACHUSETTS INFANTRY, C. 1830

USNM 60355–M (S–K 111). Figure 132.

This silver-on-copper plate bears the familiar elements of the Massachusetts seal: Indian, in hunting shirt, with bow in right hand, arrow with point downward in left hand, and star above right shoulder. The crest—an arm grasping a broad sword on a

wreath of the colors—is superimposed on a burst of sun rays above. The State's motto is written around the shield. The earlier plates containing elements of state arms were for the most part confined to the States of Massachusetts, Connecticut, and New York. No large plates bearing Pennsylvania State symbols that can be dated prior to 1835 are known.

This seal was not authorized by law until 1885. However, the devices and the motto were elements of the seal of the Commonwealth of Massachusetts ordered prepared by the state legislature in 1780 and, although apparently never formally approved, used as such for many years. It differs considerably in detail from the seal in use from 1629 to 1684.[109]

CAP PLATE, MASSACHUSETTS INFANTRY, C. 1835

USNM 60316–M (S–K 72). Figure 133.

This scalloped plate, which is struck in thin iron metal and silvered, bears elements of the Massachusetts seal, minus the motto, and the legend "MASSACHUSETTS MILITIA." Its silver color assigns it

---

[109] See ZIEBER, pp. 141–144.

FIGURE 133

to the infantry. The form of the specimen indicates that it was probably designed prior to 1839. In consideration of its over-all design and the use of the word "MILITIA," it was probably made as a stock pattern and sold to several different organizations. A plume holder, which has been resoldered to the reverse, appears to be of the same metal as the plate proper. It is pierced at the sides for attachment.

¶ Painted cap fronts were worn during the War of the Revolution by several units of the Continental Army—including the Light Infantry Company of the Canadian Regiment, Haslet's Delaware Regiment, and the Rhode Island Train of Artillery [110]—and it is probable that the practice continued among some volunteer corps up to the War of 1812. Their use in the uniformed Militia units generally declined after the introduction of die-struck metal cap plates. Two notable exceptions are a cap plate of the Morris Rangers that is attached to a civilian-type round hat

of the 1812–1814 period [111] and the cap front described below (fig. 137).

Although discarded by the more elite volunteer corps, painted metal hat fronts in the "tombstone" shape similar to that of the Morris Rangers continued to be used, to some extent, by the common Militia. Easily attached to the ordinary civilian hat of the period, they provided the common Militia a quick and inexpensive transformation from civilian to military dress at their infrequent musters perhaps as late as 1840. There are several contemporary sketches of these musters and in one, dated 1829 (fig. 134), these "tombstone" plates can be identified.

A total of perhaps a dozen of these hat fronts are known. Most are of Connecticut origin, although at least two containing New York State devices are extant. The most elaborate of these devices bears, oddly enough, elements of the Connecticut State seal, the motto *Qui Trans. Sust.*, and the crest of the Massachusetts coat of arms—an arm grasping a broadsword (fig. 135). The elaborate detail of this plate indicates that it was probably an officer's. The fact that unit designations on other such known hat fronts run as high as the "23d Regt." is definite proof that these were devices of the common Militia as opposed to the volunteer corps.

PAINTED CAP FRONT, CONNECTICUT, C. 1821
USNM 604764-M (S–K 909).   Figure 136.

This painted front, of leather rather than metal, forms an integral part of the cap itself. Edged in gold, it has the unit designation "LIGHT INFANTRY: 2d COMP." in gold at the top; a shield in the center contains elements of the Connecticut State seal, and below it is the state motto "QUI TRANS SUST" ("He who brought us over here will sustains us").

CAP FRONT, C. 1830
USNM 60243-M (S–K 1).   Figure 137.

A majority of these hat fronts are very similar in design, size, and shape, and are painted over a black background on thin precut sheets of tinned iron. This specimen carries a gold eagle with the Federal shield on its breast and a ribbon in its beak. The unit

---

[110] Illustrated in LEFFERTS, pls. 4, 7, 21.

[111] In the collections of the Morristown National Historical Park. The Morris Rangers was one of three uniformed Militia units in Morris County, New Jersey, at the outbreak of the War of 1812; it saw service at Paulus Hook in 1814 (HOPKINS, pp. 271–272).

THE NATIONS BULWARK.

A well disciplined Militia

Pub. for the Proprietors by R.H.Hobson, Chesnut St. Philad.ª 1829

FIGURE 134.—From Library of Congress print.

FIGURE 135.—Specimen in Campbell collection.

FIGURE 137

FIGURE 136

ment; and 1st Company, 8th Regiment. The plate shown here has metal loops soldered to the reverse close to the edge midway between top and bottom for attachment to a civilian type hat by means of a ribbon or strip of cloth. Other such plates have hole for attachment with string.

CAP PLATE, SOUTH CAROLINA, C. 1835–1850

USNM 60318–M (S–K 74).   *Figure 138.*

This crescent-shaped, silver-on-copper plate bears an eagle that is very similar in design to the one adopted by the Regular Army in 1821. Sometimes mistakenly identified as a gorget because of its shape, the crescent form of the specimen is an old South Carolina State heraldic device. A cap worn by the Charleston Light Dragoons after the Civil War, and

designation, "2d comp^Y. 23d reg^T.", also in gold, is below. The artwork, although somewhat unartistically executed, has an attractive simplicity. Other such hat fronts in the national collections are of the 2d Company, 6th Regiment; 3d Company, 6th Regi-

FIGURE 138

probably before, carries a similar crescent-shaped plate, with the familiar palmetto tree device substituted for the eagle.[112] The design of the eagle, however, places this piece in the 1835–1850 period. A silvered ornament, it may have been made originally for either infantry or dragoons, and must be considered a manufacturer's stock pattern.

CAP PLATE, WASHINGTON GRAYS, C. 1835

USNM 60251–M (S–K 9).   Figure 139.

This brass, diamond-shaped plate was worn by the Washington Grays, a light artillery outfit of Philadelphia. Within a raised oval are a profile of Washington—with his shoulders draped in a toga, a typically neoclassic touch—and, below, the unit designation "GRAYS" in raised letters. A matching oval shoulder-belt plate struck from the same die is known.[113]

Many Militia units named themselves after prominent military personalities. There were Washington Guards, Washington Rifles, Jackson Artillerists, and so forth.

---

[112] Illustrated in *Military Collector and Historian* (1951), vol. 3, no. 3, p. 59.

[113] See *U.S. Military Magazine* (April 1839), pl. 5.

72

FIGURE 139

CAP PLATE, NATIONAL GREYS, C. 1835

USNM 60291–M (S–K 49).   Figure 140.

An illustration in *U.S. Military Magazine* [11] shows this plate being worn by the National Greys; however, with such a nondistinctive center ornament as the rosette of six petals, it must surely have been a stock pattern sold to many different organizations. The sunburst proper is struck in brass, as is the rosette, and each of the rays is pierced at the end for attachment. The rosette is affixed with a brass bolt, also for attachment, which must have extended through the front of the cap.

CAP PLATE, ARTILLERY, C. 1840–1850

USNM 60333–M (S–K 89).   Figure 141.

This plate is struck in very thin brass. The combination of devices in the design, especially of the

---

[114] May 1839, pl. 7.

cannon and cannon balls, indicates that it was probably made for Militia artillery. Its shape suggests that it may have been worn high on the cap front, with the sunburst serving an added function as a cockade of sorts. It was very probably a stock pattern.

CAP PLATE, MOUNTED TROOPS, C. 1836

USNM 60319–M (S–K 75). *Figure 142*.

From the size of this brass plate it can be assumed that it was worn without other ornament on the front of the round leather cap associated with mounted troops. The upper portion of the shield bears 8-pointed stars, an unusual feature. The arrows in the eagle's left talon point inward, a characteristic of eagle representation between 1832 and 1836. The plate is known both in brass and with silver finish. It was probably a stock pattern issued to both cavalry and mounted artillery.

CAP EAGLE, C. 1836

USNM 60391–M (S–K 147). *Figure 143*.

This brass eagle was worn in combination with backgrounds of full-, half-, and three-quarter sunbursts and as a single ornament on the cap front. The inward-pointed arrows in the left talon place it in the 1832–1836 period. Known in both brass and silver-on-copper, it was a popular stock pattern sold to many units.

CAP PLATE, C. 1836

USNM 60381–M (S–K 137). *Figure 144*.

Struck in copper, and silvered, this eagle, which is very similar in design to that prescribed for the Regular Establishment in both 1821 and 1832, was made for Militia infantry from about 1836 to perhaps as late as 1851. Specimens struck in brass are also known, and the same eagle is found on half-sunburst backgrounds. It is quite possible that this is the eagle illustrated in the Huddy and Duval prints as being worn by both the Washington Blues of Philadelphia and the U.S. Marine Corps.[115]

CHAPEAU ORNAMENT, C. 1836

USNM 60287–M (S–K 45). *Figure 145*.

This brass ornament is a die sample or unfinished badge. After the circular device was trimmed from

↑ FIGURE 140   FIGURE 141 ↓

---

[115] *U.S. Military Magazine* (February 1840), pl. 28; (November 1840), unnumbered plate.

FIGURE 142

the brass square, it would have been worn as an officer's chapeau ornament or as a side ornament on the round leather dragoon cap of the period. The four arrows in the eagle's left talon are unusual.

CHAPEAU COCKADE, GENERAL OFFICER, C. 1840

USNM 604962–M (S–K 1106). Figure 146.

This large, round chapeau cockade with its gold embroidery and sequins on black-ribbed silk and its ring of 24 silver-metal stars appears to be identical

FIGURE 143

to cockades that have been shown as being worn around 1839 by Gen. Edmund P. Gaines and Gen. Winfield Scott [116] but without the added center eagle. Close examination of this cockade shows it to be complete, with no traces of a center eagle ever having been added. The 24 stars would have been appropriate at any time between 1821 and 1836.

CAP AND CAP PLATE, JACKSON ARTILLERISTS, C. 1836

USNM 604780 (S–K 925). Figure 147.

The Jackson Artillerists of Philadelphia, after the appearance of the regular dragoon cap plate in 1833 and the large crossed cannon of the regular artillery one year later, lost no time in combining these two devices to make their distinctive cap device.[117] It seems probable, however, that the plate was adopted by other artillery units and eventually became more or less of a stock pattern.

CAP PLATE, WASHINGTON GRAYS(?), C. 1836

USNM 604608–M (S–K 755). Figure 148.

The Washington Grays of Philadelphia wore a diamond-shaped plate with a likeness of George

[116] *U.S. Military Magazine* (May 1841), unnumbered plate; (March 1841), unnumbered plate.
[117] Illustrated in *U.S. Military Magazine* (January 1840), pl. 26.

74

FIGURE 144

FIGURE 145

Washington in the center (see fig. 139), but this plate, for some other "Washington" unit, bears his likeness in silver metal on a brass sunburst background. This silver outline of the head of Washington is also known on cartridge-box flaps of the period.

CAP PLATE, ARTILLERY, DIE SAMPLE, C. 1836

USNM 60288–M (S–K 46). Figure 149.

This uncut, brass cap plate may have been a manufacturer's die strike sent out as a sample, with others, so that a distant Militia organization could select a pattern. The finished plate is known on a bell-crown cap of the pattern of the 1820's, but its design indicates that it probably should be dated after 1834 when the Regular artillery first adopted the crossed-cannon device. The eagle is distinctly similar to the one adopted by the Regulars in lieu of cap plates in 1821, and the modified sunburst background probably was taken from the 1833 dragoon device.

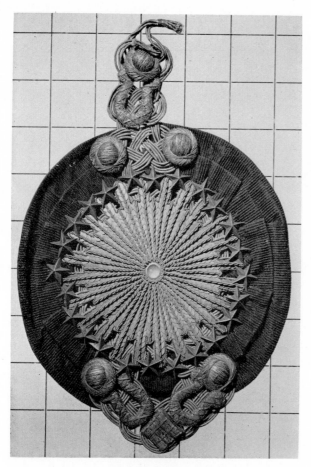

FIGURE 146

FIGURE 147

CAP PLATE, C. 1836

USNM 60292–M (S–K 50). Figure 150.

This cap plate is a somewhat wider variation of the 1833 dragoon device than most of the Militia plates of that type popular in the late 1830's and the 1840's. While the brass sunburst has the usual 8-pointed form, the eagle, applied to the center, is unusually small (1⅜ by 1 in.) and gives every indication of having been originally designed as a cockade eagle at a somewhat earlier period.

CAP PLATE, C. 1836

USNM 60274–M (S–K 32). Figure 151.

This pattern of the 1833 dragoon eagle on a half-sunburst, struck in brass and silvered, was worn by the Washington [D.C.] Light Infantry [118] and possibly by other units of the period. Both the eagle and the half-sunburst were obviously stock items.

[118] Illustrated in *U.S. Military Magazine* (August 1839), pl. 15.

FIGURE 148

76

FIGURE 149

FIGURE 150

FIGURE 151

FIGURE 152

FIGURE 153

CAP PLATE, REPUBLICAN BLUES, C. 1836

USNM 604606 (S–K 753). Figure 152.

This silver-metal plate can be accurately identified by reading its devices. The center device is from the seal of the State of Georgia. During the period that the plate was worn, one of the best known of the State's Militia organizations was the Republican Blues—the "RB" on the plate—of Savannah.[119] The silver color of the plate also agrees with the other trimmings of the uniform of that unit.

CAP PLATE, IRISH DRAGOONS, C. 1840

USNM 604605 (S–K 752). Figure 153.

This three-quarter-sunburst plate with the monogram "I D" applied in silver is identical to one on a brass-bound dragoon cap in the national collections carrying in its crown the label "Irish Dragoons, Brooklyn, N.Y." (USNM 604691, S–K 837). It is typical of the two-piece sunburst-type plates and was probably worn until the 1850's. The plate was attached by means of two looped-wire fasteners that were run through holes in the helmet and secured by leather thongs.

---

[119] A volunteer Militia company known as the Republican Blues was organized in Savannah in 1808. From notes filed under "Georgia National Guard" in Organizational History and Honors Branch, Office of the Chief of Military History, Department of the Army, Washington, D C.

CAP AND PLATE, LANCER TYPE, C. 1840

USNM 604688–M (S–K 834). Figure 154.

With no regulations but their own to restrain them, Militia organizations designed their uniforms to suit their fancies, although generally following the regu-

FIGURE 154

lations for the Regulars. This often led to odd and unusual cap shapes and trimmings and bindings on clothing, and to somewhat garish horse furniture in in some mounted units.

The illustrated cap and plate is very similar to the ones worn by the Boston Light Infantry[120] about 1839–1840 except that the upper or "mortar board" portion is beige instead of red and the plate is a full instead of a three-quarter sunburst. The mortar board form is that introduced by the Polish lancers in Europe in the early years of the 19th century and worn by most European lancer reigments of the same period. Lancer units in the British Army adopted this type cap in 1816 when they were first converted from light dragoons.[121] The large, brass, eagle-on-sunburst plate was obviously patterned after the one prescribed for the Regular dragoons in 1833.

FIGURE 155

COCKADE EAGLE, INFANTRY, C. 1836

USNM 60377–M (S–K 133). Figure 155.

As an example of more than a dozen known variants of the eagle, this silver-on-copper specimen is illustrated to show the general form and size of Militia cockade eagles that became distinct types in the 1830's and continued until about 1851. All such eagles were obviously stock patterns.

COCKADE EAGLE, C. 1836

USNM 604960–M (S–K 1104). Figure 156.

This gold-embroidered cockade eagle with a wreath of silver lamé about its breast appears to have been patterned directly after the eagle on the 1833 Regular dragoon cap plate (see fig. 38). It possibly is one of a type worn by general officers of Militia. On this specimen, both the eye and mouth of the eagle are indicated with red thread.

FIGURE 156

COCKADE EAGLE, C. 1836

USNM 604959–M (S–K 1103). Figure 157.

This gold-embroidered eagle, with wings and tail of gold embroidery and gold sequins, was worn by staff and field officers, and possibly general officers, of Militia. A duplicate on an original chapeau is in the collections of the Maryland Historical Society in Baltimore, Maryland. Eagle ornaments such as this were generally centered on a round cloth cockade about 6 inches in diameter. The eagle's mouth is indicated by embroidery with red thread. Similar eagles of a smaller size are known on epaulets of the same period.

[120] Depicted in *U.S. Military Magazine* (November 1839), pl. 22.

[121] BARNES, p. 106 and pl. 2(14).

79

FIGURE 157

CAP PLATE, C. 1840

USNM 604511–M (S–K 658). Figure 158.

The flaming grenade, adopted by the Regulars in 1832 after long usage by the British and other foreign armies, was quickly adopted by the Militia. This specimen, of silver-on-copper, was worn as a cap plate either in conjunction with another device below it on the cap front or as a lone distinctive ornament. It cannot precisely be identified as an artillery plate, but since some Militia artillery units are definitely known to have worn silver buttons of the artillery pattern, such is highly probable. Also known in brass and in smaller sizes, it is a stock pattern.

CAP PLATE, C. 1840

USNM 604526 (S–K 673). Figure 159.

Although this plate appears to be of possible French or British origin, close examination indicates that it is probably an American Militia device of the 1840's. Its looped-wire fasteners indicate that it is a cap plate. The design of the modified Napoleonic-type eagle is almost exactly that used in the 1833 Regular dragoon cap plate and other Militia plates; and the period of apparent manufacture coincides with the

FIGURE 158

early use of the flaming grenade as an American device. Incorporating two devices common to the period, it would have been a stock pattern.

CAP PLATE, ARTILLERY, C. 1840

USNM 60432–M (S–K 188). Figure 160.

The 1840 button for the Ordnance Corps bears a flaming grenade over crossed cannon, devices that date from 1832 and 1834 respectively. Consequently, it seems likely that this combination emerged as a stock pattern for Militia artillery early in the 1840's. This specimen, struck from a single piece of brass, is a copy of the French artillery device of the same period, and, while it is believed to be American, it may be a foreign insignia. Confusion arises in the case of foreign designs, for die sinkers often used as a model either an actual imported badge or a scale drawing of one.

FIGURE 159

FIGURE 160

CAP PLATE, ARTILLERY, C. 1840

USNM 604548–M (S–K 695). Figure 161.

This is a variation of the pattern of the preceding specimen in which silver-metal devices have been placed on a small, gilt, half-sunburst plate. This was probably a stock pattern available to any Militia organization beginning about 1840 and worn for the next 20 or 30 years.

CAP PLATE, SOUTH CAROLINA, C. 1840

USNM 604533–M (S–K 680). Figure 162.

The palmetto of South Carolina in outline form first appeared as a large cap ornament about 1840, after having been worn in smaller size as a cockade ornament and on the side of dragoon caps. A Huddy and Duval print shows it on the caps of the DeKalb Rifle Guards of Camden, South Carolina.[122] The illustrated specimen was worn into the 1850's, and it is highly probable that some South Carolina troops wore plates such as this in the early days of the Civil War.

The palmetto was adopted as the principal heraldic device of South Carolina in commemoration of the defeat of Admiral Sir Peter Parker's fleet by the garrison of Sullivan's Island under Col. William Moultrie in June 1776. The defenses of the island were constructed primarily of palmetto logs. The devices comprising this brass plate are all taken from the state seal, including the mottos *Animis Opibusque Parati* and *Dum Spiro Spero Spes*. The date "1776" alludes to the year of Moultrie's victory and not to the organization date of any particular unit.

CAP PLATE, SOUTH CAROLINA, C. 1840

USNM 604532–M (S–K 679). Figure 163.

Struck from a different die, with broader fronds and a wider base, this brass plate is of the same period as the preceding one.

CAP PLATE, C. 1840

USNM 60295–M (S–K 53). Figure 164.

This grenadier-type plate, struck in brass, is one of the most beautiful examples of the die maker's art in the national collections. On a sunburst-over-clouds

---

[122] *U.S. Military Magazine* (August 1841), unnumbered plate

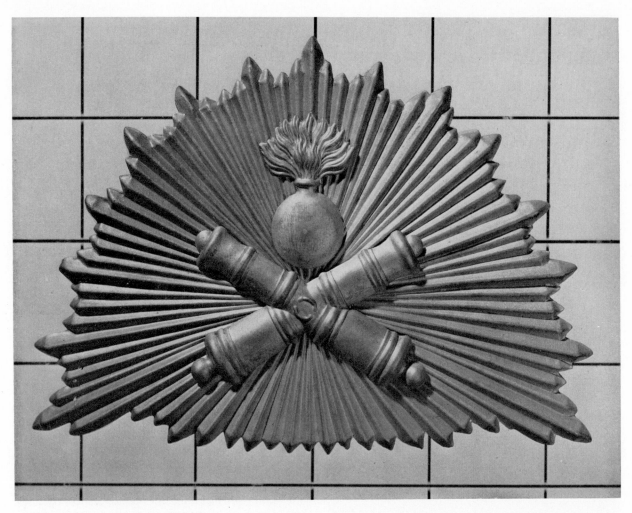

FIGURE 161

background is an eagle grasping the top of the Federal shield superimposed on panoply of arms and colors. The national motto is on a ribbon below. Certainly not from a stock pattern, this plate obviously was made for a specific Militia unit of considerable affluence. Three simple wire fasteners soldered to the reverse provide means of attachment.

This specimen is one of the scarce examples of military plates bearing the maker's name "BALE," which may be seen just above the raised lower edge and below the "UNUM." This was probably Thomas Bale of New York who is first listed in New York directories, in 1832, as an engraver at 68 Nassau Street. The 1842 directory lists him as a die sinker at the same address in partnership with a Frederick B. Smith. He is last listed in 1851.

CAP AND CAP PLATE, 1ST ARTILLERY, PENNSYLVANIA, C. 1840

USNM 604672 (S–K 819). Figure 165.

The plate on this cap uses only the shield of the Pennsylvania seal without crest or supporters. It is surrounded at the sides and bottom with a wreath carrying a ribbon with the unit designation "FIRST ARTILY." Equally interesting and unusual is the small separate insignia at the pompon socket. It is based on the 1840 flaming grenade ordnance device with crossed cannon superimposed.

COCKADE EAGLE, C. 1840

USNM 60394–M (S–K 150). Figure 166.

This eagle is of a rather odd design, and the five arrows in its left talon is an even more unusual vari-

82

FIGURE 162

FIGURE 163

ation. It is believed to be a cockade eagle because of its form and size, but it may well have been used elsewhere on the person as a piece of uniform insignia.

CHAPEAU COCKADE, STATE FENCIBLES (PENNSYLVANIA), C. 1840

USNM 60259-M (S-K 17). *Figure 167.*

The State Fencibles of Philadelphia were originally organized as "Sea Fencibles" in 1812 for duty at the port of Philadelphia. This cockade, with brass eagle, was first worn about 1840 and it continued in use for many years thereafter. Dates incorporated as parts of devices are generally the original organizational dates of the units concerned—as is the case in this instance—and bear no necessary relation to the age of the badges. Some Militia cap plates bear the date "1776," and there are waist-belt plates bearing organization dates of 100 years earlier than the dates at which the plates were made.

¶ The transition to composite plates in the late 1830's was a tremendous step forward in the field of military ornament. Handsome insignia could be manufactured less expensively and individual units were able to have plates distinctive to themselves at relatively low cost; however, only gold and silver colors could be used. In the mid-1840's there was introduced a new manufacturing technique which opened this field even wider. In this innovation, various stock patterns were struck with a round center as a part of the design. In either the initial strike, or a second, this round center was punched out, leaving a hole. Then pieces of colored leather or painted tin—carrying distinctive numerals, letters, monograms, or other devices were affixed to the reverse of the plate, in effect filling the hole. Although this added a step in manufacture, it permitted the incorporation of bright colors, which added zest and sparkle to the finished product. Such plates remained popular until the 1890's, and a few are still worn on the full-dress caps of some units. This type of insignia came into use at the time when many of the independent com-

FIGURE 164

panies of the larger states, such as New York and Pennsylvania, were starting to become elements of regiments and brigades within the over-all Militia structure of the state, thus the use of distinctive numbers and/or letters on the badges. Many of these units, however, retained their original designation [123] and continued to wear insignia distinctive to themselves on full-dress uniforms.

CAP PLATE, 1845–1850

USNM 604559–M (S–K 706). *Figure 168.*

The first of the stock patterns, with basic wreath and 8-pointed starlike sunburst, has the numeral "1" on

---

[123] *New York Military Magazine* (June 26, 1841), vol. 1, no. 3, p. 45.

black leather as a center device. Other specimens in the national collections have single numerals, single letters, branch of service devices, and state coats of arms. This plate, and those following, were worn through the 1850's on the dress cap copied after the pattern adopted for the Regular Establishment in 1851. It is struck in brass.

CAP PLATE, 1845–1850

USNM 604617–M (S–K 764). *Figure 169.*

This stock pattern, in brass, is very definitely military in composition, employing cannon and flag-staff spearheads radiating from a beaded center and superimposed on a sunburst background. The metal letter "I" is backed with black leather.

FIGURE 165

FIGURE 167

FIGURE 166

CAP AND CAP PLATE, ALBANY BURGESSES CORPS, C. 1851

USNM 604681–M (S–K 827). Figure 170.

This unusually ornate and distinctive plate is that of the Albany [New York] Burgesses Corps that was founded, as stated on the plate itself, October 8, 1833. The arms and the motto "ASSIDUITY", appearing above the ribbon with the letters "A B C," are those of the city of Albany.

CAP AND CAP PLATE, RIFLES, C. 1851

USNM 604666–M (S–K 813). Figure 171.

The original buttons on the sides of this cap have the eagle with the letter "R" (used by both Regulars and

FIGURE 168

Militia) on the shield. The brass plate proper, however, includes no device indicative of any particular branch of service; combining flags and a Federal

85

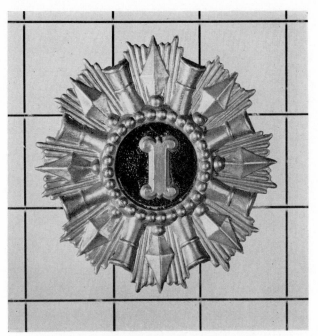

FIGURE 169

FIGURE 171

FIGURE 170

other than the numeral "1" in the eagle's beak and the letter "E" in the shield. It is a type more apt to have been made about 1850 than later. The eagle is struck in brass, and the stippled inner portion of the shield, product of a separate strike, is soldered in place; thus, the plate proper must be considered a stock pattern.

FIGURE 172

shield surmounted by an eagle, it may well have been a stock pattern.

CAP PLATE, C. 1850 (?)

USNM 604551 (S–K 698). Figure 172.

The type and form of this eagle plate give no clue to its age, or to the identity of the unit that wore it

CAP PLATE, C. 1850 (?)

USNM 604552–M (S–K 699). *Figure 173.*

A companion piece to the preceding plate, this specimen differs in that the letters "R G" and their stippled background are struck integrally with the plate proper—indicating that two dies were combined for a single strike—and in that the shield, ribbon, and numeral "1" have been silvered.

FIGURE 173

CAP PLATE, 10TH REGIMENT, MASSACHUSETTS VOLUNTEER MILITIA, C. 1850

USNM 60358–M (S–K 114). *Figure 174.*

This plate is of a type form worn on Militia dress caps prior to the Civil War. There is little doubt that plates such as this continued in use for several decades after their initial appearance. This brass specimen, surmounted by elements of the Massachusetts seal, is struck as a stock pattern for Massachusetts troops with the center left bank. The numeral "10" is applied to a black-painted metal disk affixed with simple wire fasteners.

CAP PLATE, GEORGIA, C. 1850

USNM 604545–M (S–K 692). *Figure 175.*

This plate and the one following are of Militia types worn on caps in the 1850's and perhaps earlier.

Such plates are known to have been in use with little or no change almost to the present day on military school dress shakos and dress caps worn by some National Guard units. The plate proper, which is of brass, is the well-known half-sunburst device so popular in the 1830's and 1840's. The Georgia state seal, also in brass, is applied with wire fasteners.

FIGURE 174

The plate is dated later than a similar one of the Republican Blues (fig. 152) because of the "feel" of the piece and the fact that it cannot be ascribed to a particular unit whose existence can be dated.

CAP PLATE, VIRGINIA, C. 1850

USNM 604547–M (S–K 694). *Figure 176.*

This plate differs from the preceding one only in that it substitutes the coat of arms of Virginia for that of Georgia. The backgrounds, although very similar, are products of different dies.

FIGURE 175

Shoulder-Belt and Waist-Belt Plates

WAIST-BELT PLATE, 1ST MARINE ARTILLERY, 1813

USNM 60323–M (S–K 79).   Figure 177.

Undoubtedly one of the most interesting of all the Militia plates of the War of 1812 period is this rectangular one worn by John S. Stiles of (as indicated by the engraving) the "First Marine Artillery of the Union." Engraved in brass, it bears an unusual combination of military and naval devices—the familiar eagle-on-cannon of the Regular artillery and the eagle with oval shield that appears on naval officers' buttons of the period.[124] Actually, the devices befit the character of the organization. The following

---

[124] JOHNSON, vol. 1, pp. 40, 74.

quotation from *Niles Weekly Register* of Baltimore, June 26, 1813, tells something of the unit:

The First Marine Artillery of the Union, an association of the masters and mates of vessels in Baltimore, about 170 strong all told, assembled on Sunday last and proceeded to the Rev. Mr. Glendy's church in full uniform, where they received an address suited to the occasion; which, as usual-done honor to the head and heart to the reverend orator. We cannot pass over this pleasant incident without observ, ing that the members of this invaluable corps are they who, of all other classes of society, feel the burthens and privations of the war.

Obviously, this organization was one of the state fencible units enlisted for defense only, but little else is known about it. In 1814 there was in Baltimore, a Corps of Marine Artillery commanded by a Capt. George Stiles. The roster of this unit, however,

FIGURE 176

FIGURE 177

does not include the name John S. Stiles. Other records do indicate that a Lt. John S. Stiles commanded a section of the Baltimore Union Artillery at the Battle of North Point in 1814.[125] It is probable that John Stiles, originally a member of the 1st Marine Artillery of the Union had transferred his commission to the Baltimore Union Artillery.

¶ An example of Militia officers' shoulder-belt plates of the period 1812–1816 is a solid silver oval plate (fig. 178) engraved with an eagle and elements of the arms of Massachusetts within a shield suspended from the eagle's neck. Being silver, the plate probably was worn by infantry or possibly dragoons. Many such

[125] SWANSON, pp. 253, 382.

FIGURE 178.—Specimen in Campbell collection.

FIGURE 179

plates were locally made, as was this one, and examination of a number of specimens gives reason to believe that many were made by rolling out large silver coins into thin ovals, which were then engraved and fitted with fasteners on the reverse. The fasteners on all pieces studied indicate that the plates were intended to be ornamental rather than functional.

In the Pennsylvania State Museum there is a similar oval plate that was worn by Col. Philip Spengler of that State's Militia in 1812–1816. Ornamented with an eagle, with the initials "PS" within an oval below, it generally follows the construction of the illustrated plate, differing only slightly in size. Since plates of this general type were made locally by hand, each is unique in itself. Identification must depend upon an interpretation of the devices engraved on the face. The initials of the officer for whom the plate was made are often included.

SHOULDER-BELT PLATE, C. 1812

USNM 604310-M (S–K 466). Figure 179.

A second example of a Militia officer's plate is this engraved brass specimen with the design placed along the longer axis of the oval. Since there probably were many "Volunteer Rifle Companies," it is impossible to determine precisely which one wore this plate. The initials of the officer may be read either "I. B." or "J. B.," for many of the early-19th-century engravers used the forms of the letters "I" and "J" interchangeably. The two small hooks on the reverse indicate that the plate was for a shoulder belt rather than for a waist belt, and that it was ornamental rather than functional.

SHOULDER-BELT BUCKLE, C. 1812(?)

USNM 60325–M (S–K 81). Figure 180.

This brass buckle, obviously made for a sword hanger, has an eagle in flight above, a 13-star flag below, and four 5-pointed stars on either side. The spearhead on the pike of the flag is definitely of military design, and, in the absence of nautical devices in the engraving, the buckle must be considered an army item.

ORNAMENTED WAIST-BELT PLATE, 1812–1825(?)

USNM 604122–M (S–K 278). Figure 181.

Cast in silver and then carefully finished, this rectangular plate with beveled edge is one of the most ornate and beautiful known. In the center is an officer's marquee with an eagle, wings spread, perched on top. In front of the marquee are a fieldpiece with bombs, cannon balls, and drum; the whole on grassy ground and superimposed on a trophy of colors and bayonetted muskets. The canton of one color has, instead of stars, an eagle with a shield on

90

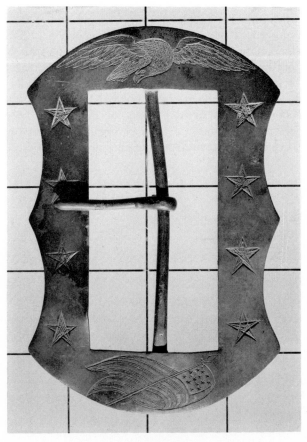

FIGURE 180

FIGURE 181

such design are known to have been used as early as the last year of the Revolution.[127] In addition, the "feel" of the specimen is early, and it is included here as a possible Militia dragoon officer's plate since the dragoons of the War of 1812 period generally wore their swords attached to a waist belt rather than to a shoulder belt.

WAIST-BELT PLATE, INFANTRY, 1814–1825 (?)

USNM 60449–M (S–K 205). Figure 182.

This plate is typical of the early waist-belt plates, which generally were more square than rectangular. It bears the over-all design of the 1814–1821 series of "common" cap plates. Struck in copper and silvered, it would have been appropriate for either infantry or dragoons, as both wore "white metal" trimmings during this period. There are as many die variations known for this type belt plate as for the matching cap plates.

The wide latitude allowed officers in selecting their own insignia makes it quite possible that this design was worn by some officers of the Regular Establishment, particularly those in the high-numbered regiments, which were organized during the course of the War of 1812. A third use of this basic design is indicated by a museum specimen at Fort Ticonderoga, N.Y.: cut into its outline form, it was worn on the side of Militia dragoon caps.

FIGURE 182

its breast and a ribbon in its beak. It has been suggested that the eagle-in-canton flag would tend to date the piece after 1820 when many Militia units had the design in its colors;[126] however, flags of

---

[126] The national collections contain several such Militia colors.

[127] See WALL.

WAIST-BELT PLATE, INFANTRY, 1814–1825(?)

USNM 60451–M (S–K 207). Figure 183.

This brass plate is one of several similar examples made of both brass and silvered copper that differ only in small die variations and the use of either 5-pointed or 6-pointed stars. The arc of 17 stars in this specimen may or may not be significant, because there were 17 states in the Union from 1802 until 1812 when Louisiana was admitted. Not until 1816 did the 19th state, Indiana, come into the Union. After thinking in terms of and working with 17 stars for a 10-year period, die sinkers may well have overlooked

FIGURE 183

the inclusion of a star for Louisiana. Buttons for the Regular rifles made after 1812 but before 1821 show an arc of 17 stars.[128] As in the case of the preceding plate, there is a good possibility that this one was worn by Regular officers in 1814–1821. It is also probable that the pattern was made and sold to Militia for many years after 1821.

WAIST-BELT PLATE, MILITIA ARTILLERY, C. 1821–1840(?)

USNM 60453–M (S–K 209). Figure 184.

While this plate could have been worn by an officer of the Regular artillery in the period 1814–1821

[128] JOHNSON, vol. 1, p. 61.

when uniform regulations were vague and seldom enforced, it is more probable that it was a Militia item of about 1821–1835. The reason for this is that the eagle-on-cannon device was adopted quickly by Militia units when it was discarded by the Regulars in 1821, and the overall design of the plate itself follows the pattern adopted by the Regulars in 1821 (see fig. 68). Several artillery organizations of the Massachusetts Militia wore the discarded button

FIGURE 184

pattern (eagle-on-cannon with the word "CORPS" below) until the 1840's,[129] and this plate would have been an ideal match.

The whole is cast in brass, the inner ring rather crudely so. The outer ring is embossed with zig-zag fretwork enclosing a circle of 5-pointed stars; the rectangular belt attachments have a floral design.

WAIST-BELT PLATE, MAINE, C. 1821

USNM 604123 (S–K 279). Figure 185.

This plate, struck in copper, contains the basic devices of the State of Maine seal enclosed by a curled ribbon border embellished with 5-pointed stars. The specimen is more square than rectangular, a characteristic of waist-belt plates of the early 1800's. It was probably worn by Maine Militia no later than the 1820's, possibly a few years earlier. The method of attachment also is indicative of this early period: the heavy vertical wire is brazed to one end of the reverse, and the L-shaped tongue to the other. This plate obviously was a stock pattern.

[129] JOHNSON, vol. 1, pp. 161, 162.

FIGURE 185

WAIST-BELT PLATE, C. 1830

USNM 60329-M (S-K 85). Figure 186.

This plate, cast in brass, is typical of the small plates, both round and rectangular, that were worn with light-weight, full-dress staff swords. It is an example of the early, hand-made, bench-assembled types. The outer ring carries the wreath typical of the period, while the inner ring carries the eagle with its head to the right, shield on breast, arrows in left talon, and olive branch in right talon. The whole lies within a ring of 13 5-pointed stars; the uppermost five stars are mixed with a sunburst rising from the eagle's wings.

FIGURE 186

WAIST-BELT PLATE, C. 1821 (?)–1830

USNM 60466-M (S-K 222). Figure 187.

This brass, bench-assembled plate is similar to the Regular artillery belt plate of 1816 (fig. 56) in that the design on the inner ring is struck with a series of separate hand-held dies on a piece of blank round stock. The floral design on the belt attachments is cast. In many of the early bench-made plates, the final assemblyman marked the matching pairs so that they could readily be re-paired after buffing and plating. In this specimen, each ring bears the numeral XXVIII.

FIGURE 187

WAIST-BELT PLATE, NEW YORK, C. 1830

USNM 60467-M (S-K 223). Figure 188.

This plate, with the center ring struck in medium brass and the belt attachment cast, was worn by Militia of New York State, as indicated by the eagle-on-half-globe device taken from that state's seal. Of brass, it is assigned to the artillery. The quality of the belt to which it is attached and the ornateness of the plate itself indicate that it was made for an officer. The left-hand belt attachment is missing.

WAIST-BELT PLATE, C. 1830

USNM 60470-M (S-K 226). Figure 189.

This small, cast-brass plate is another example of the plates made for social or full-dress wear with the light-weight staff sword. The design on the inner ring is unusual in that the eagle, with upraised wings, is standing on the Federal shield. The plate is a bench-made product, with the inner and outer rings

FIGURE 188

FIGURE 190

bearing the numeral VII. It was very probably a stock pattern for officers.

WAIST-BELT PLATE, C. 1836

USNM 60414–M (S–K 300). Figure 190.

Rather unusual in construction, this small silver-on-copper rectangular plate was struck in thin metal. Two broad tongues, for attachment to a belt, are inserted in the rear; and the reverse is filled with lead to imbed the fasteners. The eagle design is very similar to the one prescribed for the caps of the Regular Establishment in 1821, although somewhat reduced in size. The general lack of finish and polish in construction indicates that the specimen was

probably the product of an inexperienced and small-scale manufacturer.

OFFICER'S WAIST-BELT PLATE, C. 1837

USNM 60326–M (S–K 82). Figure 191.

This unusually large plate, which is struck in medium brass and with the edges crimped over a heavier piece of brass backing, is believed to be an officer's plate because of its size, gilt finish, and over-all ornate design. Within a floral and star pattern border, the specimen is dominated by an eagle, on a sunburst background, that holds in its left talon five arrows with points inward; above are 25 stars and an edge of clouds above. Arrows held with points inward are usually considered indicative of the general period

FIGURE 189

FIGURE 191

94

1832–1836. If the number of stars is of any significance, such dating would be correct, as the canton of the National Colors contained 25 stars from 1836 to 1837. The central design used without the border is also known in smaller, more standard sized plates. The design is a stock pattern. This type plate is also known in both brass and silver.

SHOULDER-BELT PLATE, WASHINGTON GRAYS, C. 1835

USNM 604348–M (S–K 504).   Figure 192.

This may well be a companion piece to the diamond-shaped cap plate ascribed to the Washington Greys[130] of Philadelphia (see fig. 139). In any case, the two appear to have been struck from the same die. It

FIGURE 192

may also have been worn by the Washington Greys of Reading, Pennsylvania, or by another company of the same designation. The specimen is struck in thin brass with a tin backing applied before the strike and the edges crimped over the reverse. Three soldered copper-wire staples provide means of attachment.

---

[130] The spelling of "Grays" may or may not be significant. A Huddy and Duval print of the Washington Greys in *U.S. Military Magazine* (April 1839, pl. 5) used "Greys" in the title and "Grays" on an ammunition box in the same print.

¶ Militia organizations generally modeled their uniforms rather closely on those of the Regular Establishment; of course, there were certain exceptions, notably the flamboyant Zouave units. However, the Militia often added additional trimmings that gave the "gay and gaudy" touch for which they were noted. Following the example of the Regulars, the Militia adopted coat-skirt ornaments almost immediately after their appearance in 1832. They used the regulation flaming grenades, open and looped horns, and 5- and 6-pointed stars, but in both gold and silver on varicolored backgrounds and in a wide variety of sizes. They also used a number of peculiarly Militia forms, such as crossed-cannon, elements of state seals, and devices peculiar to specific units.

COAT-SKIRT ORNAMENT, ARTILLERY, C. 1836

USNM 604961–M (S–K 1105).   Figure 193.

Typical of Militia coat-skirt ornaments is this pair of crossed cannon devices for Militia artillery. They are of gold embroidery on a background of black velvet. Similar pairs in the national collections are embroidered in silver. The Regular artillery never wore the crossed cannon device on the skirt of the coat; so used, it was exclusively a Militia ornament.

FIGURE 193

COAT-SKIRT ORNAMENT, SOUTH CAROLINA, C. 1836

USNM 604963 (S–K 1107).   Figure 194.

Another coat-skirt ornament with an even more distinctly Militia touch is this small palmetto tree of

FIGURE 194

FIGURE 195

gold embroidery, with sequins, on black wool cloth. As the palmetto tree is the basic device of the South Carolina seal (see pp. 81 and 83), this specimen must be attributed to the Militia of that state.

¶ Most Militia cartridge-box plates made in the decade after 1841 were oval, following the pattern of the Regulars. While a few of these varied from the prescribed sizes, most were almost identical in both size and shape to those of the Regular Establishment, but with strictly Militia ornamentation. The exact years in which these plates were produced cannot be determined, but it is reasonably sure that they were supplied to Militia for some years prior to the opening of the Civil War. Not included here are similar types known to have been made for units born of the war as the Pennsylvania Fire Zouaves, Pennsylvania Home Guard, Pennsylvania Reserve Brigade, and the Ohio Volunteer Militia. Cartridge-box and waist-belt plates often are identical except for the methods of attachment. The plates for cartridge boxes have two wire loops imbedded in the backing (see fig. 90), while those for waist belts have one or two round, or sometimes arrowheaded, prongs on one side of the reverse, and with a narrow tongue on the opposite side bent parallel to the plane of the plate (see fig. 91).

CARTRIDGE-BOX PLATE, C. 1841

USNM 60400–M (S–K 156). Figure 195.

This brass, oval cartridge-box plate, with its eagle on **a** panoply of arms and colors, closely matches in size

the 1841 Regular cavalry's plates for carbine cartridge boxes and the infantry's waist belts. Although plates of this design were worn as waist-belt plates, the two looped-wire fasteners on the reverse of this specimen clearly indicate its use on a cartridge box. This was undoubtedly a stock pattern. An oil painting of Capt. George Bumm, Pennsylvania State Artillery, c. 1840, shows the subject wearing a waist-belt plate of this same design.[131]

CARTRIDGE-BOX PLATE, C. 1841

USNM 60401–M (S–K 157). Figure 196.

Slightly smaller than the preceding specimen, this brass plate bears the eagle design popular from 1821 to 1851. Fitted with looped-wire fasteners, it would have been a stock pattern for cartridge boxes.

CARTRIDGE-BOX PLATE, MAINE, C. 1850

USNM 60354–M (S–K 606). Figure 197.

A frequently misidentified plate is this brass-struck, lead-filled oval with the raised letters "VMM" for Volunteer Maine Militia. It is also known in a smaller size. The reverse is fitted with the two looped-wire fasteners normal to such plates.

Other prewar oval plates bearing raised letters are known for the Alabama Volunteer Corps (AVC), North Carolina (NC), South Carolina (SC), State of New York (SNY), and New Hampshire State Militia (NHSM). Many such plates recently have been reproduced for sale, and more probably will be made

---

[131] *Old Print Shop Folio*, p. 216.

96

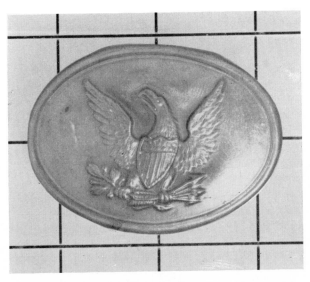

FIGURE 196

if a market is created. Thus, all plates of this general type should be cautiously considered.

WAIST-BELT PLATE, DIE SAMPLE, C. 1840

USNM 60354–M (S–K 110). Figure 198.

One of the more unusual forms of the militant eagle used on ornaments is shown on this brass die sample for a waist-belt plate. The eagle, with fierce mien and wings outspread, stands high on a craggy ledge. An example of an untold number of odd and unusual pieces of insignia, this specimen is unidentified as to unit or area of intended use. It may well have been designed for use as a stock pattern.

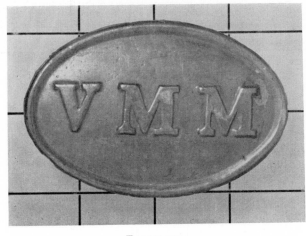

FIGURE 197

FIGURE 198

WAIST-BELT PLATE, RIFLEMEN, C. 1840

USNM 604103–M (S–K 259). Figure 199.

A stock pattern, this plate is struck in brass with the open-horn device of riflemen, which has been previously discussed. Wire fasteners are on the reverse. Although the outer ring of the plate is missing, it was probably decorated with a wreath, a common form in the 1830's and 1840's.

FIGURE 199

WAIST-BELT PLATE, CHARLESTOWN ARTILLERY, C. 1840

USNM 604385–M (S–K 532). Figure 200.

This 2-piece, brass-cast plate was worn by members of a Charlestown, Massachusetts, unit. The date

97

FIGURE 200

"1786," as on nearly all dated pieces of insignia, refers to the date of original organization of the unit. The design of the plate is typical of early- to mid-Victorian taste.

WAIST-BELT PLATE, MASSACHUSETTS, C. 1840

USNM 60497–M (S–K 253). Figure 201.

Bearing elements of the seal of the State of Massachusetts, this plate likely was a stock pattern sold to many officers. In construction, it is a composite piece similar to the plate for officers of the Corps of

FIGURE 201

Topographical Engineers (see fig. 87 and p. 45) with the device applied to the inner oval. Because of its unusually striking appearance, it would have been a most appropriate type for staff and field officers, and possibly general officers.

WAIST-BELT PLATE, NEW YORK, C. 1840

USNM 604126–M (S–K 282). Figure 202.

This plate, struck in poor-quality, medium-weight brass, is of a stock pattern bearing the eagle-on-half-globe device and the motto "Excelsior" from the New York State seal superimposed on a panoply of arms and colors. This type of belt plate, with the device on the inner panel and a wreath between the inner and outer borders, is most characteristic of the 1840's. More than ten different plates are known that vary only as to the design of the inner panel; some contain New York State heraldic devices, and others contain variants of the usual eagle design of the period.

FIGURE 202

WAIST-BELT PLATE, PHILADELPHIA, C. 1840

USNM 604390 (S–K 537). Figure 203.

The devices on this cast-brass plate comprise the arms of the City of Philadelphia, and its form and pattern, especially the floral design of the outer ring, place it in the 1840's. The piece is bench-made and carries on the reverse many marks of the file used in its final assembly. It must be considered a stock pattern.

WAIST-BELT PLATE, SOUTH CAROLINA, C. 1840

USNM 604241–M (S–K 397). Figure 204.

Somewhat larger than many plates of the period, this brass specimen carries the South Carolina palmetto device. Such plates also were struck in copper and silver plated. It obviously was a stock pattern

98

FIGURE 203

FIGURE 205

sold to several different units. The rectangular plate with the vine-patterned border was a stock pattern in itself, with many different devices being added in the center as ordered. This is one of the many pieces of insignia too often called Confederate but which antedate the Civil War by almost two decades.

FIGURE 204

WAIST-BELT PLATE, C. 1840

USNM 604388–M (S–K 535). Figure 205.

The eagle device on this silver-on-copper specimen closely resembles that on the cap plate of the First Troop Philadelphia City Cavalry (USNM 604964–M) and may possibly be the matching belt-plate worn by

that organization. Such an eagle, however, would have been a stock pattern of the manufacturer, and sold to many different units. A very unusual aspect of this particular eagle are the three arrows held in the left talon: two of them point inward, the third outward.

WAIST-BELT PLATE, ARTILLERY, C. 1840

USNM 604106–M (S–K 262). Figure 206.

Although members of the artillery of the Regular Establishment wore the crossed-cannon device on their shakos, they never wore it on waist- or shoulder-belt plates. Thus, this cast-brass plate must have been

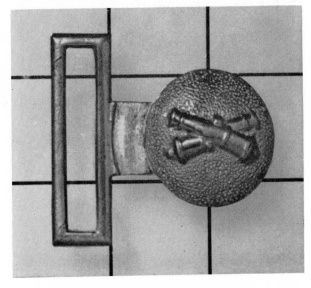

FIGURE 206

99

a stock pattern sold to many Militia units. The outer ring is missing.

WAIST-BELT PLATE, C. 1840

USNM 604107–M (S–K 263). Figure 207.

This specimen, roughly cast in brass and gilded, is unusual because the Militia rarely used the letters "U S" on any of its equipment. The pattern does not conform to anything prescribed for Regulars and the quality does not come up to standards required by the Regular Establishment; hence it must have been worn by Militia. It would have been a stock pattern. There is the possibility that it might have been worn by diplomatic personnel, but its poor quality makes this unlikely.

FIGURE 208

WAIST-BELT PLATE, C. 1840

USNM 604458–M (S–K 605). Figure 209.

The generalities that apply to all "stock pattern" insignia are equally valid in referring to this brass-struck plate with a 5-pointed star as its sole ornament. Dating its period of design poses no difficulty, for it contains the panel with wreath inside an edging border characteristic of the 1840's. The star device would have been appropriate for Militia units of Maine ("North Star"), Texas ("Lone Star"), or for dragoon units that took the star as a distinctive insignia. Although it may have been worn by Texans, it is doubtful that it was made originally for them.

FIGURE 207

WAIST-BELT PLATE, C. 1850

USNM 604387–M (S–K 534). Figure 208.

The over-all design of this plate, which is cast roughly in brass and gilded, reflects the growing ornateness of the Victorian era. Obviously a stock pattern, it would have suited the fancy of several units and cannot be identified further than "for Militia." The design of the eagle is unusual in that three arrows are carried in the right talon—although it is possible that this is intended to reflect the belligerency inherent in the period of the War with Mexico—and there is a single large star in the canton of the Federal shield.

FIGURE 209

100

The design enjoyed a long life, and plates of this general pattern were struck well into the 1880's. The major difference between earlier and later specimens is that the early ones were struck on rather heavy sheets of copper-colored brass, with fasteners consisting of a tongue and heavy wire loops brazed to the reverse. The later plates have a bright brassy color, are struck on thin brass, and have the loop and tongue soldered rather than brazed.

WAIST-BELT PLATE, C. 1840

USNM 604108–M (S–K 264). Figure 210.

The lack of a mane on the beast on this plate marks it as a tiger. The best known and most affluent Militia organization with the nickname "Tigers" was the Boston Light Infantry, although a number of others also were so-called. The craftsmanship and general elegance of this gold-plated brass specimen suggests that it was worn by an officer, though an occasional volunteer company was so richly endowed that all its members, officers and enlisted men alike, wore expensive devices. The bench-assembled manufacturing technique, gaudy embellishment, and lack of a distinct Victorian touch date the piece about 1840. The tiger's head is applied.

FIGURE 211

The unit continued to wear this plate for about half a century. While that unit's cap plate (fig. 170) is much more formal and is without a lion's head, its buttons contain the lion—with head turned to half-right—as a principal ornament. While it is probable that the original die for this cast-brass plate was sunk for the Albany organization, the manufacturer would not have hesitated to offer it for sale to any interested Militia unit.

WAIST-BELT PLATE, C. 1840

USNM 60479–M (S–K 235). Figure 212.

The raised letters "w g" on this cast-brass and gilded plate would have been suitable for many

FIGURE 210

WAIST-BELT PLATE, C. 1840

USNM 604104–M (S–K 260). Figure 211.

The full-flowing mane on the beast on this plate identifies it as a lion. The device would have been appropriate for wear by the Albany Burgesses Corps, which, when founded in 1833, almost immediately adopted the lion's head as its distinctive insignia.

FIGURE 212

101

Militia units of the period. We can only suggest that it may have been worn by members of a "Washington Greys" or "Washington Guard" from Pennsylvania or New York. A round plate with an outer wreath would have been more appropriate for officers than for enlisted personnel.

WAIST-BELT PLATE, WASHINGTON GREYS, C. 1850

USNM 604137–M (S–K 293). *Figure 213.*

The waist-belt plates shown in the *U.S. Military Magazine* [132] for the Washington Greys of Philadelphia and Reading, Pennsylvania, while indistinct, are definitely not of this pattern. Thus, this brass plate with its sunken letters filled with black enamel must have been worn by yet a third unit with such a name. Additional specimens in the national collections have the company letters "G" and "K."

FIGURE 214

FIGURE 213

WAIST-BELT PLATE, C. 1840

USNM 604294–M (S–K 450). *Figure 214.*

This oval, convex, brass plate, with two studs and a hook soldered to the reverse for attachment, very probably was originally a shoulder-belt plate. The letters "W L G" incised on the obverse are very patently the added work of an engraver of no great talent. The letters doubtless stand for Washington Light

Guard, and, since there were several Militia units of that designation, it seems possible that one of the less affluent units bought the plates and had them engraved locally.

WAIST-BELT PLATE, CITY GUARDS, C. 1840

USNM 604386–M (S–K 533). *Figure 215.*

There were City Guards in Charleston, South Carolina, New York City, Philadelphia, and possibly in other places. Thus it is impossible to determine just which of these units wore this cast-brass plate. The ornamented outer oval is typical of the 1840's.

WAIST-BELT PLATE, NATIONAL GUARD, C. 1850

USNM 60206–M. *Figure 216.*

A number of Militia units carried the designation "National Guard." The unit that used this particular plate was from New Jersey, for scratched on the reverse is "Sergeant O. Clinton, October 9th, 1851, 1st Reg Hudson Brigade, NJSM"; However, the adjutant general, State of New Jersey, was unable to give any information on such an organization. The specimen is cut from rolled brass with sunken letters filled with black enamel.

¶ Shoulder-belt plates underwent the same transition as cap plates did beginning about 1837–1838, with the single die strike plate yielding to the composite plate, and applied devices being attached to oval, rectangular, or rectangular "clipped corner" plates. While some single die plates were made and worn

[132] April 1839, pl. 5; June 1839, pl. 10.

FIGURE 215

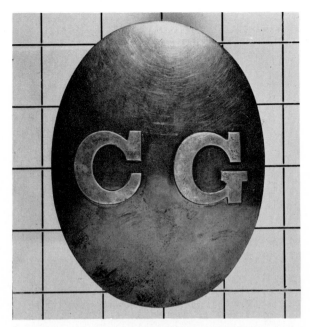

FIGURE 217

FIGURE 216

after 1840, no composite types that predate 1835 are known. The following group of shoulder-belt plates are typical of those that first appeared about 1840. Of these, several continued unchanged through the Civil War and into the 1870's and 1880's.

SHOULDER-BELT PLATE, C. 1840

USNM 604341–M (S–K 497). Figure 217.

This unusually large, oval, brass plate with the letters "c g" in silver applied with wire fasteners is another of that sizable group of lettered insignia that cannot be attributed definitely to a particular organization. The "c g" may stand variously for City Guard, Cleveland Greys, Charleston Guard, or some other organization. With a stock of oval and rectangular blanks and a set of lettering and number-cutting dies, an almost limitless combination of plates could be turned out by a single manufacturer.

SHOULDER-BELT PLATE, NEW YORK, C. 1840

USNM 604470–M (S–K 617). Figure 218.

The basic form of this brass plate—with one of the many variations of the seal of the State of New York [133] applied with wire fasteners—is a copy, with minor changes, of the bevelled plate prescribed for the Regular Establishment in 1839. Distinctly an officer's plate, it would have been appropriate for artillery or staff.

SHOULDER-BELT PLATE, C. 1840

USNM 604331–M (S–K 487). Figure 219.

This composite plate, struck in brass, has a bevelled, rectangular base almost identical to the base of the 1839 regulation plate (see fig. 86). The design consists of a silvered center ornament comprising a trophy of flags, a sword, and a liberty pole surmounted by a wreath of laurel inclosing fasces and a Federal shield with 26 stars in its canton. This silver ornament is applied with four simple wire fasteners rather than

---

[133] ZIEBER, p. 166.

FIGURE 218

basic strike, or the plate could be struck a second time to add a device integral to it. Thus the background portion of the specimen must be considered a stock pattern. A print of the National Guards of Philadelphia in *U.S. Military Magazine* for October 1841 shows an officer wearing a similar plate. If the stars are significant, the plate can be dated between 1837 and 1845.

SHOULDER-BELT PLATE, C. 1840

USNM 604471–M (S–K 618). Figure 220.

In this plate, the center ornament used in the preceding specimen has been struck directly in a rectangular, bevelled background. However, the background of this plate has a stippled surface rather than a sunburst. An interesting feature is that there are four slots punched through the plate for the attachment of an additional device over the wreath and shield. This is another of the many examples of how a unit might have an insignia distinctive to itself at little extra cost. This plate is obviously of a stock pattern. The national collections also contain a die sample of this particular plate.

FIGURE 219

FIGURE 220

soldered. Since the sun rays in the background radiate outward not from the center but from the edge of a circle about 1½ inches in diameter, almost any desired center ornament could have been added to the

SHOULDER-BELT PLATE, C. 1840

USNM 604472–M (S–K 619). Figure 221.

Another example of the rectangular, bevelled-edged, shoulder-belt plate for officers is this brass-cast copy

FIGURE 221

FIGURE 222

of the 1839 Regular Army pattern with the wire-fastened letters "s v g" substituted for "u. s." The specimen bears a touchmark "W. Pinchin Philad" on the reverse (see p. 33). The unit for which this plate was made is unidentified.

SHOULDER-BELT(?) PLATE, C. 1840

USNM 604394–M (S–K 541). *Figure 222.*

The silver letters "s f" applied with wire fasteners to the small brass plate are most appropriate for the State Fencibles of Philadelphia, and it is believed to have possibly been worn by that unit in the 1840's. A print in the *U.S. Military Magazine* [134] portraying this unit shows an officer wearing a plate of an entirely different design, but since a plate in this simple form would most probably have been worn by enlisted personnel, and the soldier in the print is to be seen only from the rear, such identification as to unit may be correct.

SHOULDER-BELT PLATE, BOSTON LIGHT INFANTRY, C. 1840

USNM 604339–M (S–K 495). *Figure 223.*

This unusually large silver-on-copper plate with its brass letters "b l i", "1798", and brass tiger's head

[134] March 1839, pl. 2.

is attributed to the Boston Light Infantry. The applied devices are attached with simple wire fasteners. The date 1798 is believed to be the year of the original organization of the unit, but the adjutant general of the Commonwealth of Massachusetts was unable to verify this.

FIGURE 223

105

SHOULDER-BELT PLATE, NEW YORK LIGHT GUARD, C. 1840

USNM 604351–M (S–K 507). Figure 224.

The *New York Military Magazine* provides us with a strong clue in identifying this clipped-corner, bevelled-edged brass plate with a silver-on-copper tiger's head applied. In a sketch of the Light Guard of New York it is related that, following a visit in 1836 to the Boston

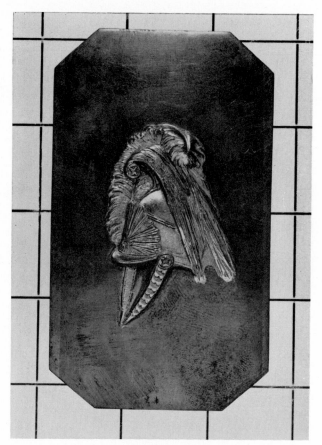

FIGURE 225

FIGURE 224

Light Infantry, members of the company "adopted, as part of their uniform, a silver tiger's head, to be placed on the breast plate, as a further memento of the spirited and elegant corps whose guests they had been." [135] This specimen is in agreement with that description.

SHOULDER-BELT PLATE, DRAGOONS, C. 1840

USNM 604352–M (S–K 508). Figure 225.

An unusual manufacturing technique was used in making this plate. It was struck in very heavy brass about $\frac{1}{16}$ inch thick and the whole tinned; then, all the tin on the obverse, except that on the crested

---

[135] *New York Military Magazine* (1841), vol. 1, p. 118.

helmet device, was buffed away, giving the center ornament the appearance of having been silvered. The specimen obviously was made for a particular mounted unit, designation unknown. An interesting detail is the letter "A" on the half-sunburst plate of the dragoon helmet device.

SHOULDER-BELT PLATE, C. 1840

USNM 604350–M (S–K 506). Figure 226.

This plate, which is of brass with a cast, white-metal likeness of Washington applied with wire fasteners, may well have belonged to either the Washington Greys of Philadelphia or the unit of the same designation of Reading, Pennsylvania. Prints of these two organizations in *U.S. Military Magazine* [136] show profiles on the shoulder-belts plates, although the plate of the Reading unit is depicted as being oval.

---

[136] April 1839, pl. 5; June 1839, pl. 10.

SHOULDER-BELT PLATE, C. 1840

USNM 604337–M (S–K 493). Figure 227.

This brass plate with its wire-applied devices obviously belonged to an Irish-group Militia unit. The Huddy and Duval print of the Hibernia Greens of Philadelphia [137] definitely depicts an Irish harp on both the shoulder-belt plate and the cap plate, but the motto "ERIN GO BRAGH" is not included. The specimen would have been suitable for several Militia organizations, such as the Irish Jasper Greens of Savannah, Georgia, and the Montgomery Hibernia Greens. Its devices are wire-applied, and it possibly was a stock pattern.

SHOULDER-BELT PLATE, C. 1840

USNM 604340 (S–K 496). Figure 228.

This plain brass plate, having wire-applied pewter letters "S L I" is believed to have been worn by the Salem Light Infantry of Massachusetts.

SHOULDER-BELT PLATE, NEW ENGLAND GUARDS, C. 1840

USNM 604343–M (S–K 499). Figure 229.

Letters signifying the New England Guards are embossed on a shield of white metal that is attached to this brass plate, which has scalloped corners. Although the officer depicted in the Huddy and Duval print of the New England Guards [138] wears a waist belt rather than a shoulder belt for his sword, the soldier standing in the background is shown with crossed shoulder belts. Thus, this plate may have been an item of equipment for enlisted personnel rather than for officers.

SHOULDER-BELT PLATE, MASSACHUSETTS, C. 1840

USNM 604342–M (S–K 498). Figure 230.

Although the white-metal arm and sword on wreath device wired to this large brass plate immediately identifies the origin of the specimen as Massachusetts, the considerable heraldic license taken by this insignia-maker is only too evident. When the Massachusetts State seal was first adopted in 1780, the blazonry of the crest was given as follows: "On a Wreath a dexter Arm cloathed and ruffled proper,

---

[137] *U.S. Military Magazine* (January 1840), pl. 27.
[138] *U.S. Military Magazine* (November 1839), pl. 21.

FIGURE 226

FIGURE 227

FIGURE 228

FIGURE 229

grasping a Broad Sword . . . ."[139] The designer has placed the arm in armor and replaced the "broad sword" with a scimiter-like, edged weapon. The use of the crest of a state seal or coat of arms to indicate the state was common usage, with the eagle-on-half-globe of New York providing an excellent example. This plate would have been appropriate for wear by any Massachusetts unit, and is thus considered to have been a stock pattern.

FIGURE 230

SHOULDER-BELT PLATE, SOUTH CAROLINA, C. 1840
USNM 604454–M (S–K 601).   Figure 231.

The silver palmetto tree identifies this as a South Carolina plate. The letters "L" and "A" are subject to several interpretations, the more probable being "Light Artillery." The devices are attached with simple wire fasteners, and the basic brass plate can be considered to have been a stock item adaptable to any number of units.

[139] ZIEBER, pp. 143–144.

108

FIGURE 231

SHOULDER-BELT PLATE, C. 1845

USNM 60357–M (S–K 113). *Figure 232.*

This brass, lead-backed badge bears no devices that would assist in identifying it as to unit, and its general composition would have made it appealing to more than one Militia organization. It is considered a stock pattern. The stars-on-belt motif, forming the border of the oval, is very unusual, as are the 14 arrows in the eagle's left talon and the star beneath its beak. The

center eagle device is applied with simple wire fasteners.

¶ Following the War with Mexico, many State Militia, especially those in the south, began using their state coats of arms as the principal devices on their waist-belt plates. The plates for officers followed the earlier pattern for Regulars, a round device clasped within an outer ring. Plates of enlisted personnel more often were rectangular, but there were many exceptions. The following series includes examples of both types.

WAIST-BELT PLATE, ALABAMA, C. 1850

USNM 604221–M (S–K 377). *Figure 233.*

The old Alabama State seal with a representation of a map of the State hung from a tree trunk, as depicted on the inner ring of this cast-brass waist-belt plate, became obsolete after the Civil War when the "reconstruction" government changed the device to that of an eagle resting on a Federal shield. Some years later, however, the original seal, in somewhat modified form, was readopted. Although made in the early 1850's, plates of this type were worn by personnel of the Confederate States Army throughout the Civil War. Many plates of this same basic pattern were made in England and run through the blockade.

FIGURE 232

FIGURE 233

WAIST-BELT PLATE, CALIFORNIA, C. 1850

USNM 604389–M (S–K 536). *Figure 234.*

The 31 six-pointed stars in the outer ring of this cast-brass plate bearing the central elements of the

FIGURE 234

FIGURE 236

California State seal indicate that it was made after statehood was granted in 1850 but before 1858 when Minnesota became the 32d State. Actually, this design for the arms of the State was adopted in anticipation of admission to the Union, on October 2, 1849.[140] The ornate design of this plate is more characteristic of the 1840's than later, indicating that it was made very early in the 1850's.

WAIST-BELT PLATE, FLORIDA, C. 1850

USNM 604224-M (S-K 380). *Figure 235.*

The palm tree, standing alone, although sometimes mistaken for the palmetto of South Carolina, is representative of the State of Florida. Thus, this plate is ascribed to Florida Militia, about 1850. The

FIGURE 235

---

[140] ZIEBER, p. 114.

110

late Richard D. Steuart, of Baltimore, Maryland, an outstanding authority on Confederate equipment and accoutrements, was firm in asserting that this pattern should be ascribed to Florida.

WAIST-BELT PLATE, MASSACHUSETTS, C. 1850

USNM 604124-M (S-K 280). *Figure 236.*

While cast-brass plates of this type were first made in the early 1850's, their use continued for 20 years or more after that decade. The principal device on this specimen is taken from the arms of the Commonwealth of Massachusetts. The form of the plate is identical to the pattern of the eagle-wreath plate adopted by the Regulars in 1851.

WAIST-BELT PLATE, C. 1845

USNM 604244-M (S-K 400). *Figure 237.*

The star device was used by the Militia of both Texas and Maine, as well as by volunteer units located in other states; thus, this plate cannot be ascribed to any particular geographical area. Plates such as this, with the silver wreath of laurel and palm, are patterned directly after the basic plate prescribed for officers of the Corps of Engineers in 1841. They would have been stock items for general sale.

WAIST-BELT PLATE, C. 1850

USNM 604242-M (S-K 398). *Figure 238.*

This cast-brass officer's plate, a pre-Civil War product of American manufacture, would have been ap-

FIGURE 237

FIGURE 238

FIGURE 239

propriate for wear by Texas Militia. Obviously a stock pattern, it would also have been sold to Militia organizations in other parts of the country. As in the case of most round plates, the outer ring is of a standard design; variation in pattern would occur on the inner ring.

WAIST-BELT PLATE, NEW YORK, C. 1850

USNM 604125–M (S–K 281). Figure 239.

This brass-struck rectangular plate carries the arms of the State of New York [141] with its familiar eagle-on-half-globe device. The whole is superimposed on a sunburst background. The plate originally was made for Militia, but it is conceivable that such a plate may have been worn by early uniformed police.

WAIST-BELT PLATE, NEW YORK, C. 1850

USNM 60487–M (S–K 243). Figure 240.

This brass-cast plate with its letters "s n y" for State of New York is copied directly from the 1836 plate for noncommissioned officers of the Regular Establishment. The example is the oldest known use of the letters "s n y" for New York Militia. In later patterns, the letters "s n y" and "n y" were placed on rectangular plates and on oval plates worn on the waist belt and on cartridge boxes just prior to and during the Civil War. Small square plates with silver, Old English letters "NY" are included in the 1900 catalog of the Warnock Uniform Co. of New

FIGURE 240

[141] For the variations in the arms of New York see ZIEBER, pp. 166–167.

York as regulation pattern that year for National Guard officers.

WAIST-BELT PLATE, NEW YORK CITY, C. 1850

USNM 604141–M (S–K 297). Figure 241.

This cast-brass plate bears the arms of the city of New York superimposed on an almost full sunburst. The surrounding wreath of laurel is taken directly from the plate authorized for general and staff officers of the Regular Establishment in 1832. While this is thought to be the plate for the New York City Guards, for whom a matching shoulder-belt plate is known, there is the possibility that it was also worn by uniformed police of the 1850's.

FIGURE 242

FIGURE 241

WAIST-BELT PLATE, C. 1850

USNM 604393–M (S–K 540). Figure 242.

A stock pattern, this cast-brass and gilded plate would have been appropriate for any of the several organizations called "National Guards" or "National Greys" that existed in a number of states. The letters "N G" do not connote the National Guard as we know it today.

WAIST-BELT PLATE, OHIO, C. 1850

USNM 604136–M (S–K 292). Figure 243.

The center piece applied to this cast-brass plate with wire fasteners bears an early form of the arms of the State of Ohio.[142] The plate proper has holes in it other than those needed to apply the present device, which indicates that it was a stock part, or

---

[142] For an interesting discussion of the evolution of the arms of Ohio see PREBLE, pp. 639–642.

112

FIGURE 243

possibly that the present center device is not origina to the plate.

WAIST-BELT PLATE, OHIO, C. 1850

USNM 604130–M (S–K 286). Figure 244.

This plate bears another variation of the Ohio State arms. Here, the arms lie within a wreath as prescribed for Regular general and staff officers in 1832. The entire specimen is cast in brass; the wreath, sun, arrows, canal wall, and hull of keelboat are silvered.

WAIST-BELT PLATE, PENNSYLVANIA, C. 1850

USNM 60474–M (S–K 230). Figure 245.

Officers of the Pennsylvania Volunteer Militia wore plates of this type in the 1850's, although most were

FIGURE 244

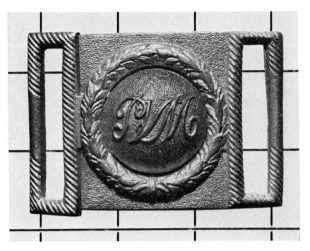

FIGURE 245

discarded in 1861 when Pennsylvania troops went into active Federal service. The outer ring, with floral wreath design, has been modified to give the appearance of a solid rectangle. Another plate in the national collections bears the letters "P V M" with the conventional outer ring.

WAIST-BELT PLATE, C. 1850

USNM 60480–M (S–K 236). *Figure 246.*

Just prior to 1850 there were two Militia units in Philadelphia using the letters "P G" to indicate organizational designation—the Philadelphia Guards and the Philadelphia City Greys. This brass-cast plate is believed to have been worn by the Philadelphia Guards, whose buttons were marked "P G." The buttons worn by the Philadelphia City Greys carried the three letters "P C G." [143]

WAIST-BELT PLATE, PROVIDENCE MARINE CORPS ARTILLERY, C. 1850

USNM 604147–M (S–K 303). *Figure 247.*

The letters and device on this rather unusual brass plate make its identification easy. The letters stand for the Providence [R.I.] Marine Corps Artillery; the date 1801 is the unit's original organization date. The crossed cannon indicate Militia artillery. The letters and numerals are of white metal and brazed to the plate. The brass crossed cannon are affixed with wire fasteners. The reverse is fitted with a broad tongue and two wire hooks for attachment.

---

[143] JOHNSON, vol. 1, p. 145, vol. 2, pl. 63.

FIGURE 246

WAIST-BELT PLATE, SOUTH CAROLINA, C. 1850

USNM 604455–M (S–K 602). *Figure 248.*

Although this specimen is not so old as the similar South Carolina plate described previously (fig. 162), it is believed to date about 1850. The plate proper is of rolled brass, and the applied device, which comprises well-known elements of the arms of South Carolina, is struck in brass and attached by means of two wire staples and leather thongs.

WAIST-BELT PLATE, VIRGINIA, C. 1850

USNM 604253–M (S–K 409). *Figure 249.*

This plate, carrying the Virginia seal, was made about 1850 for wear by officers. Similar plates made by British manufacturers during the Civil War to

FIGURE 247

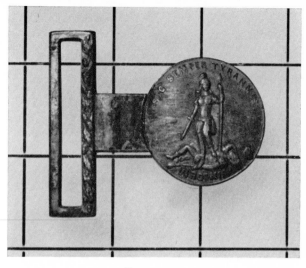

FIGURE 249

FIGURE 248

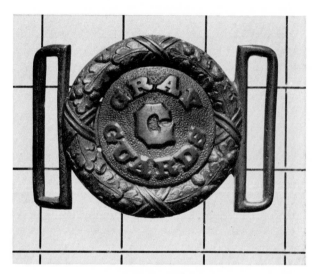

FIGURE 250

Guards." The central "G" probably indicates "Company G." The whole is cast brass.

WAIST-BELT PLATE, C. 1850

USNM 60490–M (S–K 246). Figure 251.

This plain brass plate of unusually fine manufacture is very definitely a stock pattern which could have been sold without ornament or, as was more likely, with a center device added by soldering or brazing. The plate was cast in three pieces, with the round center brazed to the belt attachment. It was bench-fitted, as indicated by the numbers on the reverse of the inner and outer rings.

be run through the blockade are generally distinguishable by their unusually sharp, clean die work. The center device of this specimen is struck in brass and brazed in place; the remainder of the plate is brass-cast.

WAIST-BELT PLATE, GRAY GUARDS, C. 1850

USNM 60489–M (S–K 245). Figure 250.

The unit for which this plate was made cannot be precisely identified. It is reasonable to assume that there were several Militia organizations called "Gray

FIGURE 251

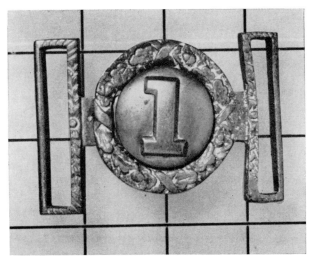

FIGURE 253

WAIST-BELT PLATE, C. 1850

USNM 60498–M (S–K 254).   Figure 252.

This is a typical stock pattern with the company designation "E." Other specimens in the national collections have the letters "D," "F," "K," and "R." Although rather crudely cast in brass, this piece has been bench-fitted and then gilded.

FIGURE 252

WAIST-BELT PLATE, C. 1850

USNM 60492–M (S–K 248).   Figure 253.

This is another stock pattern with company designation. In this case, the numberal "1" has been applied with wire fasteners rather than cast integrally with the two portions of the plate. The national

collections also contain similar plates with the numerals "2," "26," and "36."

WAIST-BELT PLATE, C. 1850

USNM 60468–M (S–K 224).   Figure 254.

This is another typical stock pattern with the eagle-on-shield device surrounded by 13 5-pointed stars as the center ornament. It is cast in brass in two pieces. An example of this plate, on a belt, formed part of a cased Sharps rifle outfit displayed at the 1960 National Rifle Association meeting in Washington, D.C.

WAIST-BELT PLATE, MUSICIAN, C. 1850

USNM 60499–M (S–K 255).   Figure 255.

The musician's lyre has never been strictly a military ornament, being widely worn by civilian bands; thus, this plate cannot precisely be identified as military or nonmilitary. Unlike most plates of this type and period, the entire piece is struck in brass rather than cast.

WAIST-BELT PLATE, C. 1850

USNM 60485–M (S–K 241).   Figure 256.

The letters "T C B" on this brass-cast plate open wide the doors of conjecture as to interpretation. Possible combinations range from Trenton City Blues (if such a Militia organization ever existed) to Troy Cornet Band, a nonmilitary unit. Plates such as this can seldom be positively identified.

115

FIGURE 254

FIGURE 257

FIGURE 255

WAIST-BELT PLATE, C. 1850

USNM 60478–M (S–K 234). Figure 257.

As in the case of the preceding plate, the letters "H R" on this specimen cannot be specifically identified. Similar unidentified plates in the national collections have the letters "S O I" and "P B."

WAIST-BELT PLATE, C. 1850

USNM 604167–M (S–K 323). Figure 258.

This plate is known both in heavy metal stamping and in thin, cheap brass. Examples of the latter type appear to have been struck in the period of the 1890's from a die then 50 years old. A plate similar to this one has been excavated from a Civil War battlefield site. A stock pattern, the design was obsolete for

FIGURE 256

FIGURE 258

116

issue to Militia before the Civil War, but it is known to have been continued almost to the end of the century for use by groups such as secondary school cadet corps.

¶ The shoulder-belt plates worn in the 1850's were little changed from those of the preceding decade. In the Regular Establishment the shoulder belt and plate for officers had been discarded in favor of the waist belt for carrying the sword, but Militia officers—bound by no regulations—continued to wear the shoulder belt. Enlisted personnel wore at least one shoulder belt, and in many cases used two belts, which crossed, one belt carrying the cartridge box and the other the bayonet and scabbard. Mounted Militia sometimes wore the saber on a waist belt and the carbine cartridge box on a shoulder belt. It is interesting to note that the custom of using elements of state seals on waist-belt plates was not followed to any great extent in the embellishment of shoulder-belt plates except in the Southern States.

CARTRIDGE-BOX-BELT PLATE, SOUTH CAROLINA, C. 1845(?)

USNM 604451–M (S–K 598). Figure 259.

In size and pattern this plate is exactly like that prescribed for the Regular Establishment in 1841, substituting the arms of South Carolina for the eagle. It possibly may date as early as 1845. Made for South Carolina Militia, plates similar to this were worn during the Civil War and several have been re-

covered from battlefield sites. The specimen is struck in brass and the reverse filled with lead. It has three bent-wire fasteners imbedded in the reverse, which indicates that it was decorative rather than functional. A similar plate with elements of the Virginia State seal is known. Modern reproductions of both are being sold.

SHOULDER-BELT PLATE, C. 1850

USNM 604446–M (S–K 593). Figure 260.

A popular stock pattern of the 1850's, this design with the silver numeral "1" on a rectangle of rolled brass was worn for at least half a century after it first appeared. Similar plates are known with all numerals through 9 and a few higher numbers. Other plates of the same general type are known with company letters "A" through "M." The plate proper is fitted with two brass wire hooks and a medium width tongue, indicating a functional use. The numeral is attached by means of two staples with leather thongs reeved through on the reverse of the plate.

FIGURE 260

SHOULDER-BELT PLATE, C. 1850

USNM 604360–M (S–K 516). Figure 261.

This rolled-brass plate with its silver "TC" monogram is presently unidentified. In the national

FIGURE 259

FIGURE 261

FIGURE 262

collections there is a Militia helmet with the same device used as part of the cap plate; also known is another insignia, comprising the monogram alone, that was used as a cartridge-box device. *New York Military Magazine* for July 17, 1841, refers to the elegant armory of the Troy [N.Y.] Corps where the Light Guard of New York had been visitors. This plate may have been an insignia of that organization. The monogram is affixed with staples and leather thongs, and the plate proper carries a large safety pin soldered to the reverse for purely decorative attachment. It is unknown whether the safety pin fasteners are contemporary with the plates to which they are attached. Rudimentary safety pins were known in Egypt before Christ, but they apparently did not appear in America until the 1830's and 1840's. Walter Hunt patented the first American safety pin in 1849.[144]

SHOULDER-BELT PLATE, C. 1850

USNM 604361–M (S–K 517).   Figure 262.

Several Militia organizations of the 1840's and 1850's were called "Republican Guards," and this silver "RG" monogram on a rolled-brass rectangle would have been appropriate on shoulder belts of so-named units. The monogram is affixed with wire

[144] U.S. Patent 6281 (April 10, 1849).

fasteners, but the means of attachment for the plate proper are missing.

SHOULDER-BELT PLATE, C. 1850

USNM 604362 (S–K 518).   Figure 263.

The silver letters "GG" on this rolled-brass plate present several possibilities for identification. Among

FIGURE 263

the uniformed Militia units of the 1840's and 1850's were Garibaldi Guards, German Guards, and Gray Guards. This piece could have been the device of any of the three. The letters are affixed with wire fasteners, and a safety pin is soldered to the rear of the plate proper for decorative attachment.

SHOULDER-BELT PLATE, C. 1850

USNM 604363–M (S–K 519). Figure 264.

This oval brass plate with the wire-affixed silver-on-copper letters "AG" is unidentified, but it might well have been worn by the American Guards, or by a uniformed company from some city as Atlanta or Albany, with the letter "G" representing "Grays," "Guards," "Grenadiers," or the like. It was attached to the belt with three simple wire fasteners.

FIGURE 265

FIGURE 264

SHOULDER-BELT PLATE, C. 1850

USNM 604335–M (S–K 491). Figure 265.

The white-metal device on this brass plate comprises elements of the arms of "New Amsterdam" topped by the crest of the arms of New York State with supporting figures representing the original Indian owner of Manhattan Island and the mariner who became the first white settler. The specimen is believed to have been worn by the New York City

Guard. The device is affixed with three staples originally intended to be reeved through with leather thongs, although now bent over. The means of attachment of the plate proper are missing.

SHOULDER-BELT PLATE, C. 1850

USNM 604364–M (S–K 520). Figure 266.

The letters "K L G" forming the white-metal monogram on this brass plate indicate that it could well have been worn by the Kentish Light Guard of Rhode Island. The monogram is attached by means of two staples with thongs reeved through, and the plate proper is fitted with four similar staples. The reverse bears the hallmark of William H. Horstmann and Sons, well-known military outfitters of Philadelphia.

SHOULDER-BELT PLATE, C. 1850

USNM 604336–M (S–K 492). Figure 267.

The white-metal letters "SG" on this brass plate lend themselves to so many interpretations that no identification is attempted. The applied device has two staples for attachment, and the plate proper is fitted with a safety pin on the reverse.

FIGURE 266

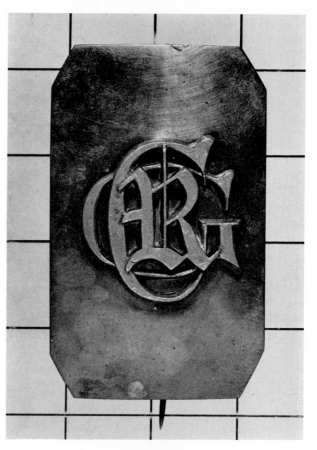

FIGURE 268

FIGURE 267

SHOULDER-BELT PLATE, C. 1850

USNM 604338–M (S–K 494). Figure 268.

Many volunteer companies used the designation "Rifle Guards," and this plate with the initials "C R G" probably falls into such a category. The

FIGURE 269

"c," of course, cannot be identified. The monogram is of pewter and has three round lugs fitted through holes in the plate proper for attachment with pins. The plate itself has a safety pin soldered to the reverse for attachment.

SHOULDER-BELT PLATE, SCOTT LEGION (?), C. 1850

USNM 604347–M (S–K 503). Figure 269.

Although this plate bearing the profile of Gen. Winfield Scott is very similar in design and construction to several bearing the head of Washington and dated much earlier, it is believed to postdate the War with Mexico when Scott's popularity was at its zenith. There were several volunteer units called "Scott Legion" during this period. The piece was struck, with a tin backing applied, and the edges of the obverse were then crimped over. It is fitted with three wire staples for attachment.

SHOULDER-BELT PLATE, C. 1850

USNM 604327–M (S–K 483). Figure 270.

This is a stock pattern in cast brass. It is oval with raised edges and has a white-metal "F" applied with simple wire fasteners. Although the piece has the appearance of a waist-belt plate or cartridge-box

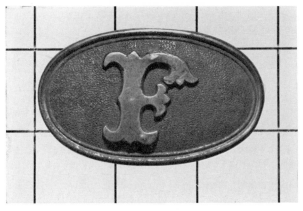

FIGURE 270

plate, the wire fasteners on the reverse indicate that it was intended for shoulder-belt wear. In the national collections is a similar plate with the letter "I," indicating that the letters designate companies of larger units rather than a unit itself.

SHOULDER-BELT PLATE, ARTILLERY, C. 1850

USNM 604356–M (S–K 512). Figure 271.

This rolled-brass plate with a wire-applied silvered "A" and pile of cannon balls topped by the hand die-struck motto "ALWAYS READY" is unidentified beyond the fact that it was worn by a member of Company A of a Militia unit using a popular motto. Similar specimens in the national collections have center letters "B," "D," and "E." The plate was attached to the shoulder belt by means of two flat brass fasteners soldered to the reverse. The fasteners are almost as wide as the plate itself.

FIGURE 271

BALDRIC DEVICE, C. 1850

USNM 60409–M (S–K 165). Figure 272.

The baldric is a highly ornamented wide sash normally worn by drum majors and sometimes by band leaders. During at least part of the Civil War, baldrics were worn by some aides-de-camp, and the 1902 uniform regulations specified them for Signal Corps officers. This specimen and the one that follows are the earlier of several examples in the national collections; they fall in the early 1850's. The shield, suspended from a lion's mouth by small chains, carries an eagle with a shield on its breast. The stars and edge of clouds, above, are somewhat similar to

121

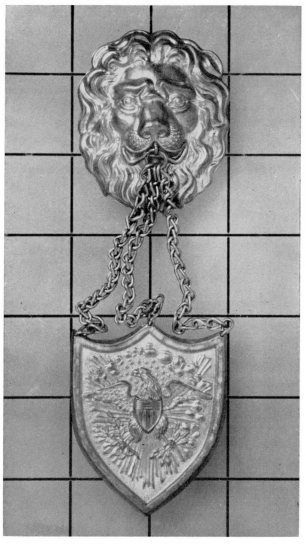

FIGURE 272

FIGURE 273

those on the 1851 regulation waist-belt plate. The whole is superimposed on a three-quarter sunburst. Both the lion's head and the shield are fitted with simple wire fasteners for attachment.

BALDRIC DEVICE AND BALDRIC, C. 1850

USNM 66622–M. Figure 273.

The device is attached to a red, gold-edged-embroidered baldric worn by the drum major of the 72d New York Militia during the Civil War but believed to ante-date 1861. The brass shield, with ebony drum sticks, is suspended from an eagle of the 1834 Regular Army pattern for wear as a cap device. The shield, convex with beveled edges, is very similar to waist-belt and shoulder-belt plates of about 1850.

¶ Few Militia gorgets are known, and this scarcity leads us to believe that few were made and worn, despite the Militia's love for the "gay and gaudy." Still, some units did adopt them, and officers of the Portland [Maine] Rifle Corps were still wearing them

122

in the late 1850's.[145] As a military symbol for officers, the gorget passed its zenith in the late 18th century. Gorgets were worn during the War of the Revolution by both American and British officers, and the British also gave them to Indian chiefs as marks of authority. Officers in at least one regiment of the Regular Establishment wore them as part of their regulation dress about the turn of the 19th century, but they were not a part of the prescribed uniform during or after the War of 1812.

GORGET, C. 1821 (?)

USNM 60311–M (S–K 67B).   Figure 274.

This gorget, of gilded brass, is of 2-piece construction. The eagle-on-clouds, very similar to cockade

FIGURE 274

---

[145] In the national collections are a uniform jacket, chapeau, and gorget once owned by Frederick Forsyth, a member of the Portland Rifle Corps in 1857.

eagles worn in 1808–1821, is attached by four wire fasteners rather than brazed. The engraved edging on the gorget proper is rather crudely done. Although composite insignia did not come into general use until the mid-1830's, it seems reasonable to assume that this particular design of the eagle device applied to the chapeau might equally have been applied to a gorget. A similar specimen in the national collections has a silver-on-copper eagle instead of a brass one.

GORGET, C. 1830–1840

USNM 60310–M (S–K 67A).   Figure 275.

This gorget is of 3-piece construction, the specimen proper being of brass and the wreath and eagle of

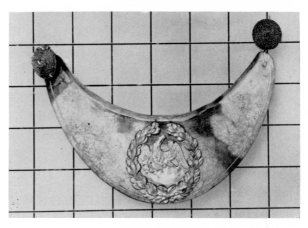

FIGURE 275

gilded brass applied with wire fasteners. Although the eagle is of the early "on-clouds" design, the feel of the piece is later, and this, together with the rather wide crescent indicate that it belongs to the period of the 1830's and 1840's.

GORGET, STATE FENCIBLES, NEW YORK, C. 1840–1850

USNM 60309–M (S–K 66).   Figure 276.

This brass gorget, with wreath and letters in applied silver, is an example of one of the later

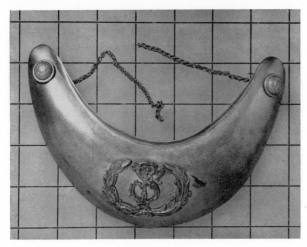

FIGURE 276

types worn by Militia. The letters "s f" are interpreted as "State Fencibles," and the "Excelsior" buttons on the ends of the crescent identify the origin of the unit as New York State. Fencibles were basically troop units organized for home defense only. There was a volunteer Militia company called the "State Fencibles" in New York City as early as 1800. It apparently lost its identity as such in 1847 or 1848 when the organization split, half entering the 8th Regiment and half entering the 9th Regiment of New York State Militia.[146]

---

[146] Personal communication from Frederick P. Todd, July 6, 1960. Mr. Todd is the foremost authority on New York Militia units.

U.S. Government Printing Office: 1963